VW TREASURES BY KARMANN

Karmann-Ghia
Beetle Convertibles
Rabbit Convertibles
Scirocco

Jan P. Norbye

Motorbooks International
Publishers & Wholesalers

© Jan Norbye, 1985
ISBN: 0-87938-202-3
Library of Congress Number: 85-15575

Printed and bound in the United States of America.
Book and cover design by William F. Kosfeld.
Cover photo by Vince Manocchi.

Motorbooks International is a certified trademark, registered
with the United States Patent Office.

1 2 3 4 5 6 7 8 9 10

Motorbooks International books are also available at discounts
in bulk quantity for industrial or sales-promotional use. For details write to Marketing Manager, Motorbooks International,
P.O. Box 2, Osceola, Wisconsin 54020.

Library of Congress Cataloging-in-Publication Data

Norbye, Jan P.
    VW treasures by Karmann.

    Includes index.
    1. Karmann Ghia automobile.   2. Karmann-Rheine
GmbH.   I. Title.
TL215.K35N67   1985   629.2'222   85-15575
ISBN 0-87938-202-3 (pbk.)

ACKNOWLEDGEMENTS

My prime objective in undertaking the writing of this book was to search out the truth about how this car actually came into being. In the past I had often been struck by the paucity of information on that subject. In some sources it was glossed over by enthusiastic talk about its beauty. Others stirred controversy.

None of the principal actors in the drama of its creation are alive today, and none, as far as I could find out, had left records that future historians could consult.

By the grace of honest and objective help, advice and information from many quarters I have been able to present what I believe is a complete and factual account of the events.

Both Wilhelm Karmann, Jr., and Gian Paolo Boano granted me the full benefit of their memories in personal interviews. My friend Dick Langworth provided material from his interviews with the Exners, father and son, and allowed me to use excerpts from articles he had written.

Filippo Sapino, general manager of Ghia Operations, opened the archives for me and allowed me to borrow freely of its drawings for publication as long as the house of Karmann had no objection. In this way I secured much illustrative material that had never been revealed to outsiders before.

Sergio Coggiola received me in his office and talked freely about his years at Ghia. And Giacomo Gaspardo Moro was able to shed new light on some questions, confirm or deny the truth of much that had been said and written about the people of Carrozzeria Ghia and their work.

Some extremely rare Ghia car photographs, on loan from the collection of Angelo Tito Anselmi, have been put into my hands by courtesy of Dr. Antonio Amadelli of Fiat's Centro Storico. Dick Langworth again came to my rescue with pictures of many Chrysler styling prototypes.

My visit to the Karmann factory and museum was organized by Herrn P. Jühe, who also was able to pull valuable information out of the Karmann archives for my use. It was Wilhelm Karmann, Jr., who agreed to release the Ghia drawings I wanted, and two Karmann engineers, Gottfried Niemann and Gerd Gieseke, told me the stories of their involvement with the Karmann-Ghia over the years.

Dr. B. Wiersch gave me free access to the Volkswagen archives, and his assistants supplied copies of hundreds of documents. All my work at Wolfsburg was facilitated by Günther Hornig and Dietmar Fritsche of the Press Department.

To all of these individuals and the organizations they work for I wish to express my most sincere gratitude. Their active help has been vital to the completion of this work, and if it fails to present some aspect of the Karmann-Ghia story in the light they would like to see it, I can only apologize and say that I have tried to balance my account equally and strictly on the strength of the available evidence, to the best of my ability.

Jan P. Norbye

CONTENTS

INTRODUCTION

One might consider the Volkswagen a notoriously unlikely basis for a sports car. The fact is that sports cars have, over the years, been developed from vehicles with less performance and roadholding potential. And don't ever forget that the Porsche pedigree starts with a humble Volkswagen chassis!

A car to feel sporty in.

This book is dedicated to the concept of the Volkswagen as a sports car, and its focal point is the models that bore the Karmann-Ghia label. Because the lines of demarcation between the Karmann-Ghias and other models, such as the VW Beetle convertibles, regarding their merits as sports cars, are vague, I devote more than peripheral attention to models that a sports car aficionado of the purest stripe would categorize as "recreational" vehicles.

It is not my purpose to redefine the term sports car. Any argument to that end would be irrelevant. But how should the VW Beetle convertible be classified? Obviously, it is not an economy sedan. It is not a family car. It is made for fun, relaxation and a driving experience giving a great sense of freedom. Its appeal was not high speed nor race-winning potential, but it made people feel sporty. To its owners, it was a sports car in the touring fashion.

Historically, the four-seater VW Beetle is particularly significant as background to the Karmann-Ghia models, for it was also produced by Karmann, and over 25,000 Beetle convertibles had been built before the Karmann-Ghia coupe went into production.

The low-priced convertible market.

Production of the Karmann-built VW Beetle convertible began in 1949, at a time when low-priced convertibles were quite common in Europe. The Nuffield group offered a Morris Minor convertible, and the Rootes group had a Hillman Minx convertible. Even better known, though more expensive, was the Singer Nine four-seater roadster. France's Renault had a 4 CV Cabriolet as a cataloged model, and Peugeot sold important numbers of its 203 two-seater convertible. Opel introduced an Olympia Cabrio-Limousine in 1950, Deutsch of Cologne had been building convertible versions of Ford Taunus since 1951 and Hebmüller produced a Hansa 1500 Cabriolet for Borgward from 1950 to 1952. It was important for Volkswagen to be present in the convertible market, and with his choice of Karmann, VW President Heinz Nordhoff secured the services of the most experienced specialist in convertible construction that western Germany possessed. Karmann's main rival in prewar days had been Gläser of Dresden, since lost to the Soviet-occupied zone in the east.

If the VW Beetle convertible was one of many folding soft-top cars more or less in the same class, the Karmann-Ghia was unique. No other mass producer had anything like it in its range of standard production models.

Unbeatable three-way combination.

The genius of its concept had three parts. The first was the use of an inexpensive mass-produced chassis of extraordinary ruggedness and reliability. The second was the hallmark of Italian styling, by one of the best-known coachbuilding and design firms, Carrozzeria Ghia. The third was the industrial solution of having the car built in northern Germany, relatively close to the Wolfsburg factory, by a firm that could be relied upon to maintain its reputation for quality above all.

With this combination, Volkswagen had a new weapon that was to have great influence as an image-builder, in addition to achieving a high degree of commercial success.

Planned daily production for the Karmann-Ghia coupe was fifty cars, and the price was set at DM 7,500 fob Osnabrück.

That was a very competitive price, matching some popular Ford and Opel sedans, and less than half the price of the Mercedes-Benz 190 SL hardtop coupe. More important, there was nothing like it on the market. The closest thing that was made in Germany was the DKW two-seater Sonderklasse Luxus-Coupe. It was almost DM 1,500 cheaper than the Karmann-Ghia, but it shared the sheet metal of the Sonderklasse sedan up to the belt line, and its hardtop-style roof recalled the two-door sedan silhouette. It was as low on marks of distinction as the Karmann-Ghia coupe, which stood in complete contrast to everything else on the VW dealers' showroom floors, was high.

The Karmann-Ghia placed Volkswagen in a privileged position vis-à-vis the public. The decision to produce this car and price it so reasonably was a bit of a gamble, but it paid off handsomely.

Absence of direct competitors.

Volkswagen also stole a march on some of its competitors for whom it would seem more natural to collaborate with famous styling studios and coachbuilders. Fiat, for instance, did not offer a sports coupe based on its 1100 (though Pininfarina produced a small series of 1100 Turismo Veloce roadsters beginning in 1954).

Renault, with *carrossiers* (coachbuilders) like Henri Chapron, Figoni, Labourdette, Antem, Guilloré and others practically in its back yard, never got around to building a sports coupe with a truly different body using the mechanical components of the 4 CV sedan.

Only Simca had a proper choice of sports coupes and convertibles based on the Aronde sedan since 1951 in its Oceane, Plein Ciel, Weekend and Coupe de Ville. But these were limited-production models with expensive bodies by Facel-Metallon, and not aimed at the same market that Volkswagen reached with the Karmann-Ghia.

Britain's major car makers had been on the track of the sports-coupe formula all along, but invariably went off in other directions, prisoners of their traditions more than anything. For instance, the Triumph 1800 Roadster of 1947 was built on the Standard Fourteen chassis (and was doomed when the Vanguard replaced the Fourteen). The Y-series and TD-type MG were engineered from the Morris parts bin, but no MG sports coupe ever came forth (until the MGB GT in 1964).

In 1949 Austin introduced the A90 Atlantic with modern but controversial styling and a price tag almost up in the Jaguar class, and followed a year later with a low-priced A40 roadster having an unattractive slab-sided body. Neither did much good for the Austin name or its earnings. The Austin-Healey of 1952 changed all that, but it was to remain an open sports car (with a ragtop).

The Singer Nine had evolved into the SM roadster by 1951, remaining faithful to the prewar styling theme, and no Singer sports coupe ever followed.

The Sunbeam-Talbot Alpine roadster of 1952 shared the sheet metal up to the belt line with the 90 sedan; and while it was a competent rally car, it was no basis for a sports coupe, as well as being outside the VW price class.

Jowett produced the Jupiter only as a roadster, sharing most of its mechanical elements with the Javelin sedan. Cars like the Riley 2½-Litre roadster and the Jaguar XK-120 were pure sports machinery and in a completely different league; as were France's last Talbot and Salmson sports coupes, Italy's Lancia Aprilia and Alfa Romeo 1900, the Mercedes-Benz 300 SL and the BMW 503 and 507.

A leader in a new class.

After the full impact of the Karmann-Ghia in the international market place had been assessed by Volkswagen's main rivals, new sports models sprouted from places where they had earlier been anathema.

Instead of exploring deals with domestic coachbuilders, Renault went to Boano of Turin for the styling of its Floride/Caravelle sports models based on Dauphine running gear. Boano had in fact been responsible for styling the Dauphine sedan, so the choice was perhaps a natural one. These Renaults did not fare too well in the market place, and did nothing to threaten the established market for the Karmann-Ghia (which became available as a convertible in August 1957).

Volvo built a small series of a plastic-bodied 444 roadster in 1956-57, before coming out with the P-1800 in 1961 (Frua of Turin had built its prototype to Swedish designs). It came very close to the Karmann-Ghia formula, using the 122-S running gear. Volvo even tried to get Karmann to build it, but Karmann did not have capacity for it, so the P-1800 was assembled by Jensen in West Bromwich until Volvo brought the operation home to Sweden.

After a few years of producing the 403 convertible, sharing the sedan's sheet metal, Peugeot went to Pininfarina for the 404 coupe and convertible, staying close to the Karmann-Ghia formula, but in a higher price bracket. With the 204 sports coupe and convertible in 1965, Peugeot came a lot closer, and probably had a more enlightened marketing policy at that time.

It was Ford that best seemed to interpret the Karmann-Ghia formula into its own production and marketing terms, coming out with the

Capri in 1961. Mechanically, it was identical to the Consul Classic, but it had its own styling theme. Yet the Classic did so poorly in the market that it earned the title of Ford of Britain's Edsel, and the Capri could justifiably be referred to as Ford's European Thunderbird. Both were quickly removed from the production program, and the Capri name was dormant from 1964 until it was brought back with a vigorously restyled coupe in 1969.

What Ford had overlooked with its first-generation Capri was that the Karmann-Ghia was based on a thoroughly successful production model, and that its styling was unanimously praised. The Capri met neither of those two prerequisites.

Original VW Karmann-Ghia production model of mid-1955 had small "nostril" air intakes, elevated Wolfsburg badge and two-tone color scheme. Its most notable innovations were the hardtop look, the curved glass all around the greenhouse, the absence of a conventional grille and the frameless door windows.

German car makers were also eagerly emulating the concept, as each could best analyze it, of the Karmann-Ghia.

Borgward made an Isabella coupe from 1957 to 1958 (and a convertible two-seater), using a maximum of the sedan sheet metal, and only its high price kept it from a successful selling career.

Auto Union produced a DKW SP-1000 coupe and convertible from 1958 to 1965. With its 55-hp three-cylinder two-stroke engine it was faster than the Karmann-Ghia, capable of 140 km/h (87 mph), but also more expensive at DM 10, 750—mainly due to its special all-steel body built by Karl Baur of Stuttgart. Auto Union also offered a series of about 100 plastic-bodied sports coupes called Monza in 1956-58, built by Fritz Wenk, a big DKW dealer in Heidelberg.

The winning combination of Volkswagen, Karmann and Ghia outlived them all. It had a production life of nineteen years with a body that never underwent radical change. The car was a phenomenon. Many examples survive in good condition, as appreciated by their owners now as the day they were bought.

Option-loaded 1955 Karmann-Ghia coupe was equipped with radio (and retractable antenna on the left side of the cowl), left-fender rearview mirror, special seat covers and whitewall tires.

Chapter One

THE VOLKSWAGEN CONVERTIBLES

Regardless of the fact that, in the planning stage, the Volkswagen was a true people's car, low-priced and austere, convertible versions were part of the project almost from the start.

The 1936 Reutter convertible.

The first VW convertible was a prototype built in 1936 on an early version of the VW chassis (Porsche Type 60). Thirty such chassis were manufactured by Mercedes-Benz under government contract for a large-scale test program, and one of them received a two-door convertible body by Reutter of Stuttgart-Zuffenhausen. The others had all-steel two-door sedan bodies.

The construction of a convertible, however, was not actually part of the government-backed People's Car scheme, but a supplementary contract from the National Association of the Automobile Industry (Reichsverband der Automobilindustrie, which corresponds to America's Automobile Manufacturers Association, now Motor Vehicle Manufacturers Association).

The Mercedes-Benz engineering department was not invited to suggest design modifications—the full design responsibility rested with the Porsche organization. Mercedes-Benz was strictly an outside supplier on this occasion.

The prototype body for the convertible did not have the final lines that were adopted for the VW Type 1 (Beetle), but borrowed design features from studies of an earlier era.

The two doors of the four-seater were hinged along the rear edge, opening at the front, as was common in low-framed cars of that time. It had one windshield wiper only (for the driver), and no bumpers were fitted. With its simple fender curves and Topolino-style wheels, it had a decidedly homemade appearance. The headlamps were mounted fairly close together on the front end sheet metal, and access to the luggage compartment was through a small near-circular lid.

With the top up, it had an angular roofline, very bulky, that made the car look old, and more than slightly reminiscent of some of the smaller Tatra models from the 1924-31 period. This car remained in Porsche's hands and did not serve as a basis for later convertible projects. Porsche destroyed it in 1942 "to keep Hitler from getting his hands on it," I was told in Wolfsburg.

The prewar convertibles.

By 1939 the Porsche organization had erected its own experimental shops at Stuttgart-Zuffenhausen, and was equipped to build small series of

Volkswagen prototype two-door, four-seater convertible, built in 1936 by Reutter of Stuttgart reveals that the Beetle shape was still in its formative stage at that time. Ferry Porsche at the wheel.

prototypes. About ninety Volkswagen preproduction cars were constructed there in 1938 and 1939.

These cars had the now-familiar Beetle body with the rounded hood, bug-eye headlamps in the fenders and eggshell roofline. The chassis design included the typical Porsche torsion-bar suspension systems, with trailing links at the front and swing axles at the rear.

The engine was a smaller version of the same air-cooled flat-four used in postwar cars. For the record, its main specifications were:

Number of cylinders	4
Bore	64 mm (2.52 in.)
Stroke	70 mm (2.76 in.)
Displacement	985 cc (60.1 cu. in.)
Compression ratio	5.8:1
Output	23.5 hp DIN @ 3000 rpm
Top speed	105 km/h (65 mph)

The Volkswagen and Porsche engineering staffs developed their own production-model convertible, which was first displayed at Wolfsburg on the occasion of the placing of the cornerstone for the new factory on May

Road-test trip in 1936 or 1937 with the Reutter-bodied convertible, in the Black Forest. Windshield carried electric-wire defroster, and side windows were removable.

26, 1938. No prices were quoted for this convertible. Advertisements from 1939 stated, in fact, that the convertible would not be part of the production program during the first years of operation at Wolfsburg. It never reached production at all, however, because the plant was converted to war materiel production. The first civilian VW's did not roll off the line until 1941, and the forty-one cars built were all Beetle sedans.

The closest thing to an open-air model in the Volkswagen 1938-39 production program was a sunroofed version of the Beetle sedan. Such cars were seen in numerous public appearances.

In KdF (Kraft durch Freude, Strength through Joy) sales literature, the sunroof-sedan was offered at a price only 60 Reichsmark above the basic price of 990 Reichsmark. Special savings coupons were planned for buyers of optional features.

VW Type 38 with full-length canvas sunroof was seen at public events in 1938. This was a parade in Munich, probably to make publicity for the VW savings scheme. Cars parked across the street are led by an Adler 2.5, Opel Admiral and Fiat 500.

Postwar convertibles.

During the war, the Wolfsburg plant turned out about 52,000 Kübelwagen (Porsche Type 82), a military vehicle with considerable off-road capability, based on the VW chassis, and 14,000 units of an amphibious version, the Schwimmwagen (Porsche Type 166), plus about 630 cars with the original sedan body. The plant was about sixty percent destroyed by the time the war ended and the British military authorities moved in. Production got under way again, slowly at first, in 1945.

Two convertibles were handmade by expert craftsmen in the Wolfsburg plant in 1947. They were two-seaters, one for Colonel C. R. Radclyffe, the military governor of the district, and one for Major Ivan Hirst of the R.E.M.E. (Royal Engineers, Mechanical-Electrical), who started off running a repair shop but ended up in charge of all facilities at the VW factory.

VW four-seater convertible prototype of 1939 shared the production-model sedan's sheet metal up to the belt line. Absence of chrome and brightwork was due to war-preparation shortages.

Operations were mainly left to Germans. The first acting manager was an engineer named Rudolf Brohrmann. He was replaced in August 1946 by Dr. Hermann Munch, a lawyer from Berlin who had no previous auto industry experience.

Josef Kales assumed the responsibilities of chief engineer. A long-time Porsche employee, he had played a major part in the design and development of the Volkswagen, and in 1941 he had been named liaison engineer between Volkswagen and Porsche.

The position of production manager was filled by Otto Hoehne, a German-American machinist who had been lured back to the Fatherland in 1938 to assist in the choice of tooling and methods for the Wolfsburg factory.

Long before the courts had decided about who actually owned the Volkswagen works, Major Hirst and Colonel Radclyffe were making preparations and plans for putting Volkswagen into a leading position in Europe's auto industry. But this could not be implemented without an experienced automotive man in charge. Colonel Radclyffe found his man in

Volkswagen's prototype convertible from 1939 became the basis for Karmann's postwar design. The mechanism, stitching and folding techniques were practically identical.

Heinz Nordhoff, who had been director of Opel's truck plant at Brandenburg (about an hour's drive from Berlin) during World War II. A spell of pneumonia saved him from the Red Army invasion, as he was convalescing in the Harz mountains when Berlin fell. The matter was quickly settled. Dr. Nordhoff went to Wolfsburg on the first day of 1948 as Volkswagen's chief executive.

The Hebmüller convertibles.

The first production-model Volkswagen convertibles had bodies by Hebmüller. Dr. Nordhoff's contact with Hebmüller came about then when the police wanted a simple patrol car on a VW chassis. There was no capacity for building it in Wolfsburg, but Hebmüller offered to do it.

Josef Hebmüller had started a wagonbuilding works at Elberfeld near Wuppertal in 1889. He soon found it necessary to set up branch factories to meet the demand, and his Wülfrath plant began making car bodies in 1919. That's where the police cars were produced.

During visits to Wolfsburg, men from Hebmüller had become familiar with the two convertibles used by the British officers, and before

Profile of the prototype Hebmüller two-seater convertible ready for an all-weather journey. Turn signal indicator was moved from the B-post to the side of the cowl.

long, talks were under way regarding production plans for a two-seater VW convertible.

About mid-year 1948, Hebmüller was engaged to do three prototypes, which were shown to Dr. Nordhoff just before Christmas of that year. He bought them, and sent them to Wolfsburg where they underwent a strict test program. A few months later, a positive report came to his desk. The way was now cleared for production, and Nordhoff signed an order for 2,000 cars.

The Hebmüller convertible had no side windows other than the door windows, for the soft top covered the whole rear quarter, right up to the B-post. The rear deck almost matched the hood in front, giving the car a well-balanced profile. When open, the soft top folded nearly flush with

Production-model Hebmüller convertible shows elegant proportions and high-grade workmanship. Rear-end modifications to the sheet metal were quite extensive.

the body at belt line level. Hebmüller had also redesigned the Beetle interior, but used as many standard VW parts as possible.

Hebmüller started production in June 1949, but the contract was never filled. Four weeks later the Wülfrath plant burned down. Rebuilding it took a long time, and the company never really got on its feet again. Production was resumed as quickly as possible, but at a dreadfully slow pace. The destruction was so great, and the insurance so inadequate, that the company never recovered from the blow. In all, Hebmüller delivered 696 two-seater convertibles.

Up to the summer of 1952, Hebmüller had produced no more than those 696 Beetle convertibles. About a dozen cars of the Hebmüller type were even built by Karmann! It was no longer a viable program, and Hebmüller discontinued VW convertible production in 1953.

Soft top on the Hebmüller convertible retracted almost completely below the belt line, making for a truly open-car appearance when folded.

A Hebmüller convertible with two-tone paint is conserved in the Karmann museum, located in the Osnabrück plant. Behind it (left) is a Karmann-built DKW convertible; on the right, an Opel Diplomat.

Like Hebmüller, Karmann also went the two-tone-paint route for the VW convertible. Karmann made greater use of the Wolfsburg sheet metal.

The Hebmüller company was then taken over by Ford, which needed production capacity; not for convertibles, but for other model variations in its expanding product range.

VW convertible by Karmann.

One day in 1948 Wilhelm Karmann, Sr., then seventy-eight years old, made a visit to Wolfsburg. He wanted to buy a car, and he had obtained the required permit. (In the immediate postwar period, customers of proven need, such as doctors, tradesmen and those employed in essential industries, were given priority for the purchase of new cars.)

Karmann did not need the car to drive it, but to modify it. It was on the merits of his new-product project that he received official approval for the purchase.

Hebmüller wanted to go into production with this VW Type 1 sports coupe, but the factory burned down before it progressed beyond the prototype stage.

Thus, while Hebmüller was preparing to build the two-seater, Karmann was already at work on the four-seater VW convertible.

Dr. Nordhoff's approval of the prototype was little more than a formality. On July 1, 1949, the same day that Volkswagen presented its first Export-model Beetle with improved body trim, fittings and equipment, Karmann announced the four-seater VW convertible. Dr. Nordhoff had signed an order for 1,000 units.

Karmann was a specialist in convertible-top body construction, but worked to strict methods of old-world craftsmanship and quality, so that by the end of the year, no more than 364 cars had been completed.

Karmann's traditions did in fact go right back to coachbuilding for horse-drawn vehicles. Its origins can be traced to 1874, when Christian Klages established a coachbuilding shop in Osnabrück. In 1901 it was taken over by Wilhelm Karmann, with a work force of eight men. The following year came the first Karmann body for a car, a Dürkopp (Dürkopp of Bielefeld in the Ruhr district had a branch factory in Osnabrück).

When Dürkopp became a regular client, others followed, such as Minerva and Opel. Karmann bodies were mainly convertibles, made with a wooden framework and steel paneling.

Karmann's folded top was a bulky affair, requiring an enormous bag-like cover, but it stole no stowage space.

By 1921 Karmann was the main body supplier to Aga, NAG and FN. Aga's first order was for 1,000 bodies, which necessitated a major expansion of the Karmann plant.

By 1927, Adler of Frankfurt was Karmann's biggest customer. Notable Karmann-bodied convertibles included the Adler Primus Cabriolet of 1932 and the Trumpf Junior Cabriolet in 1939. In 1931, Karmann began making Ford Model A convertibles, and in 1939, Karmann produced a lovely Ford Eifel convertible.

After 1945, when the demand for new convertibles was suppressed by the shortage of basic transportation, Karmann developed a healthy trade in the tool-and-die business as a supplier to Ford-Werke, Hanomag and Büssing. In later years, Karmann supplied Mercedes-Benz, Renault, Simca, Henschel, British-Leyland and Scania-Vabis with major items of body tooling.

The Volkswagen order for convertible bodies was a major step back into the firm's original production base.

Actual production of the Beetle convertible started in September 1949. The first order for 1,000 cars was filled by April 1950. VW followed

Karmann's four-seater VW convertible shared the Beetle profile to the fullest possible extent. At this time, the Beetle had a split rear window, but that was not practical for a ragtop.

through with further orders and by August 16, 1950, a full 10,000 cars had
been produced.

In the German market of 1949, the price was DM 5,450 (same as for
the Hebmüller convertible). Its success would probably not have been as
great if the price had not been so reasonable. But the amazing thing is that
celebrities and captains of industry found it a nice car to buy.

When exports to neighboring countries began, actress Brigitte
Bardot and actor Alain Delon bought Beetle convertibles. So did fashion
designers Pierre Cardin and Yves Saint Laurent. Even Gianni Agnelli
bought one (the Agnelli family controls Fiat, Turin's *La Stampa* daily news-
paper and the Juventus football team).

Instrumentation in the VW convertible was just as spartan as in the Beetle sedan. The
glovebox had no lid, and there was no fuel gauge.

SPECIFICATIONS
Volkswagen four-passenger convertible   Type 15
Valid as of February 3, 1949

Architecture

Rear-mounted engine, rear-wheel drive. Fuel tank and spare wheel between front wheels. Luggage space between front wheels and behind rear seat.

Dimensions

Wheelbase	2400 mm	94.5 in.
Track, front	1290 mm	51.0 in.
Track, rear	1250 mm	49.2 in.
Overall length	4070 mm	160.0 in.
Overall width	1540 mm	60.5 in.
Overall height (unladen)	1500 mm	59.0 in.
Ground clearance	160 mm	6.3 in.
Minimum turn diameter	11.5 m	36.0 ft.

Weight

Dry weight	780 kg	1720 lb.
Payload capacity	360 kg	794 lb.
Maximum all-up weight	1160 kg	2558 lb.
Maximum front end load	480 kg	1058 lb.
Maximum rear end load	680 kg	1500 lb.

Engine

Layout	Horizontally opposed four-cylinder with individual cylinders screwed into a common crankcase.
Cooling	Forced air: radial fan mounted on a horizontal shaft shared with the generator, and driven by V-belt from a crankshaft pulley.
Bore	75 mm 2.95 in.
Stroke	64 mm 2.52 in.
Displacement	1131 cc 69 cu. in.
Compression ratio	5.8:1
Carburetor	1 Solex downdraft 26 VFJ
Valves	Overhead, in line with the cylinder axis, operated by pushrods and rocker arms.
Valve timing	Inlet opens 17°10′ BTC
	Inlet closes 52°10′ ABC
	Exhaust opens 52°10′ BBC
	Exhaust closes 17°10′ ATC
Camshaft	Located directly below the crankshaft; driven by spur gears. Cast iron with integral cams. Base circle, 50 mm, 1.97 in.; lift, 7.45 mm, 0.29 in.
Crankshaft	One-plane forged steel, counterweighted, running in four main bearings.
Connecting rods	I-profile, forged steel, 130 mm center-to-center.
Pistons	Cast aluminum with steel insert
Output	25 hp DIN @ 3300 rpm
Torque	6.8 m-kg @ 2000 rpm

Drive train

Clutch	Single dry plate
Transmission	4-speed manual gearbox, helical gears on 3rd and 4th, no synchromesh.
Gear ratios	1st, 3.60:1; 2nd, 2.07; 3rd, 1.25; 4th, 0.80; Rev, 6.60.
Final drive	Spiral bevel
Final drive ratio	4.43:1

Chassis

Front suspension	Dual trailing links per wheel (upper and lower), with transverse laminated torsion bars and double-acting telescopic shock absorbers.
Rear suspension	Pendulum-type swing axles with trailing arms, transverse circular-section torsion bars and double-acting telescopic shock absorbers.
Front wheel rate	16 kg/cm 13.9 lb. per in.
Rear wheel rate	20 kg/cm 17.4 lb. per in.
Natural frequency under full load (cycles per minute)	83 front 77 rear
Steering	Worm-and-nut, with split track rod
Steering gear ratio	14.15:1
Overall steering ratio	17.6:1
Turns, lock-to-lock	2 7/8
Maximum steering angle	26° (outside wheel), 32° (inside wheel)
Brakes	Mechanical four-wheel system, cable-operated with eccentrics. Cast iron drums front and rear. Mechanical hand brake acting on rear drums.

Drum diameter	230 mm	9.062 in.	Acceleration	0-50 km/h (31 mph) 8.0 sec.
Lining width	30 mm	1.18 in.		0-60 km/h (37 mph) 12.5 sec.
Lining area	520 cm²	80.6 sq. in.		0-80 km/h (50 mph) 20.5 sec.
Wheels and tires	Tire size	5.00-16		0-90 km/h (56 mph) 27.0 sec.
	Rim size	3.00 Dx16		0-100 km/h (62 mph) 45.0 sec.
Dynamic roll radius	327 mm	12.9 in.	Fuel consumption	Calculated average: 6.5 liters
Inflation pressure	1.2-1.3 Bar (front) 18-19 psi,			per 100 km (36 mpg); mixed
	1.6-1.7 Bar (rear), 24.25 psi.			driving average: 7.5 liters per
				100 km (31.3 mpg)
Performance			Hill-climbing ability	1st gear, 32% gradient; 2nd,
Top speed	100 km/h	62 mph		18%; 3rd, 9%; 4th, 5%.

Ghia-bodied Alfa Romeo 6C 2500 S convertible from 1949 showed that Boano was already thinking in terms of eliminating the conventional grille, even for cars with water-cooled front-mounted engines. The air intake was integrated with the bumper —the boxes under the emblem were dummies.

Little has been said about the aerodynamic properties of the convertible (as well as the basic Beetle sedan). The fact is that the Beetle was not badly streamlined, especially when you consider that wind tunnel testing was in its infancy when Erwin Komenda designed the body, and he worked more by instinct than by precise measurement.

In recent times it has been revealed that the Beetle had an aerodynamic drag coefficient of 0.49 (which is less than it has been accused of). The same figure was valid for the convertible with the top raised. With the top folded and the side windows up, it was 0.57; and with all side windows down, 0.60.

In 1950 the Beetle line was split into Standard and DeLuxe offerings, and convertibles were built on the DeLuxe chassis. The major technical

Ghia-bodied seven-seater limousine, built 1952-53, on a Lancia Aurelia B-51 platform, showed an early application of the rear fender treatment used on the Karmann-Ghia coupe. It came from Boano's drawing board.

29

news that year included the adoption of thermostatic control for the cooling fan, the switch from mechanical to hydraulic brakes, and the installation of a heater that made less noise (though remaining relatively ineffective).

Automatic cooling airflow control by a thermostatically controlled throttle ring was also adopted for the 1950 models, and the heat riser for preheating the air-fuel mixture was first used on the 1950 engine.

On the 1951 models, the rear shock absorbers were enlarged and made double-acting. A bigger carburetor followed in 1952, as the Solex 26 VFJS was replaced by a Solex 28 PC 1. At the same time, the gearbox was redesigned with synchromesh on second, third and fourth gears, and tire size was increased to 5.60-15. The instrument panel was redesigned, and a lid was provided for the glovebox.

Ghia coupe body on Alfa Romeo 1900 C chassis, built in 1952, was the first application of Boano's front end with open air scoops on both sides of the classic grille, an idea that later showed up on some Chrysler styling prototypes.

Bigger front shock absorbers were adopted for the 1953 DeLuxe series, and the brake fluid reservoir was relocated behind the spare wheel (it was formerly mounted integrally with the master cylinder).

By 1969 the VW four-seater convertible had evolved into this shape, closely paralleling the evolution of the VW Beetle (vent windows in the doors, lights and bumpers, rear suspension).

VW four-seater convertible by Karmann, 1969 model, with the top down, shows no shrinking of either the padding or the metal mechanism for the top.

For 1954, the engine was bored out to 77 mm (3.03 inches), which increased the displacement to 1192 cc (72.7 cu. in.). The compression ratio was raised to 6.6:1, which gave higher power output and torque:

Output	30 hp DIN @ 3400 rpm
	36 hp SAE gross @ 3700 rpm
Torque	7.7 m-kg DIN @ 2000 rpm
	60.2 lb. ft. SAE gross @ 2400 rpm

It was also on the 1954 models that the dash-mounted starter button gave way to a starter/ignition key that remained in use for the rest of the Beetle's production life.

A new exhaust system with a single muffler and dual tail pipes was adopted in August 1955. At the same time, the gearshift was moved forward, and the stick bent backward to shorten the reach for first and third gears.

In the meantime, the Karmann-Ghia sports coupe had gone into production, based on the VW Export-model chassis. The further evolution of the Beetle convertible will be related in the context of the progression of sports cars joining the VW stable.

Chapter Two
ORIGINS OF THE KARMANN-GHIA COUPE

Finding the answers to the central questions regarding the creation of the first Karmann-Ghia coupe has been the most difficult part of my search for information needed to write this book.

Most of the people associated with its design are dead. I have had to sort out what I hold, to the best of my judgment, to be the truth, from a fog of guesswork, misunderstandings, wrong conclusions and false claims.

To whom does the credit for the lines of the remarkably modern and well-proportioned body belong? The striking similarity between the VW Karmann-Ghia coupe and certain Chrysler prototypes built by Ghia has raised the question of whether there was a deliberate collaboration, or whether lines drawn by one artist for one corporation were simply imitated by another stylist for use by a different client.

The Transatlantic connection.

It would be a surprise, or even a shock, for many a devoted Karmann-Ghia fancier to hear that his or her car was designed in Detroit. Was it? Some sources say it's true. According to their story, it was the work of none other than Chrysler's styling director, Virgil M. Exner, architect of Chrysler's finned "Forward Look."

This begins to sound like an industrial conspiracy worthy of treatment by fiction writers such as John Le Carre, Ross MacDonald or Arthur M. Hailey. What is there in the way of evidence to support such a notion?

Though overshadowed by the fame of industrial designers such as Raymond Loewy and George W. Walker, who were independent consultants, Virgil Exner stood out among artists employed by an auto manufacturer on a full-time basis, for his reputation went far beyond the normal confines of the industry. In the mid-fifties, when Chrysler temporarily wrested the design lead from Harley Earl of General Motors, the name Exner was almost a household word. It was even used on a car once—the imaginative but still-born Plymouth XNR prototype.

Born in 1909, Virgil Exner worked his way up in the auto design field with startling swiftness. In 1934, at the age of only twenty-five, he was named head of the Pontiac studio. His main credit at Pontiac was putting the "silver streak" on the hood and deck of the 1935 models, thereby instituting what became a mark of distinction for Pontiac through several successive styling cycles. If that seems a modest contribution, consider what he had to work with—a standard Fisher body shared with Chevrolet and Oldsmobile. "The silver streaks were all I could do when I first took over," Exner recalled later. "I thought we needed something to unify the round-top grille with the rest of the car. It worked, [but] Pontiac got themselves stuck on it, and it lasted far too long."

In 1939, Exner signed on with Raymond Loewy Studios to serve as head stylist on the Studebaker account. Here he played an important role in the design of the all-new 1947 model, though exactly how much Exner personally contributed to this epochal American car is obscure. Raymond Loewy claimed all the credit, while Exner was never mentioned officially. He left Loewy shortly afterward, and one day in 1950 Chrysler President K. T. Keller found him knocking on his door to ask for a job.

In those days, the design of the corporation's cars was dominated by its engineers. All the term styling really meant was hacking up a clay model in rough proportion to what the divisional chief engineers (and K. T. Keller) wanted. "Old K. T." always favored boxlike automobiles and the contemporary Plymouth, Dodge, De Soto and Chrysler "wouldn't knock your eyes out," as one observer quipped, "but they wouldn't knock your hat off, either."

"Ex" was given a position under Chrysler's chief stylist, Henry King. Before long, King's influence had been reduced to rubber-stamping whatever it was that Exner wanted to create, and the engineers generally went along. In just a few years, Exner transformed the whole product line.

The link between Exner and the Volkswagen was an Italian connection: Carrozzeria Ghia of Turin. Exner had been able to get corporate

Virgil M. Exner, as he looked at the time of his arrival at Chrysler Corporation. Within a couple of years, he had risen to the top post in the styling department. Did he design the Karmann-Ghia?

approval for a show-car program, cars of advanced styling to attract public attention and explore trends for future production models.

The styling quality of the Exner designs varied considerably, but all were aimed at the same goal. "There was really only a single purpose in all of them," said Exner, "and that was to let the public know that Chrysler was thinking ahead as far as styling was concerned, and doing a lot of styling exercises to search for new things and new ideas that could be put to future use."

Prototype construction was a slow and expensive job at Chrysler, and an ideal solution was found when Luigi Segre, commercial director of Ghia, made a trip to America in 1951 to look for new business.

Segre showed Exner a Ghia creation using a Plymouth chassis— the XX 500. It was designed by Mario Felice Boano, owner of Carrozzeria Ghia, and built to show off Ghia's styling ability, craftsmanship and skill, on order from C. B. Thomas, Chrysler's vice president for export.

"In retrospect," says Virgil Exner, Jr., "the XX 500 was pretty dumpy, but it was built along the lines of what they were doing in Italy at that time, the Lancia Aurelia, for instance. The design didn't scale up too well, but it started the whole idea in Dad's mind that they could do an advanced design and build it as a real car—as opposed to just mockups, as in this country."

When Exner saw the price tag for the XX 500, only $10,000, he was convinced that Ghia could provide the services he had in mind. "I jumped on the bandwagon," he said. "Eventually, K. T. Keller bought the idea as well." Luigi Segre left Detroit with a contract to build an Exner-designed body on a Chrysler chassis, and prospects for a continuing order flow.

Though Ghia was better known for its styling than as an industrial subcontractor, there was no thought at that time of using Ghia as a design consultant. The Chrysler show cars were Exner designs, and Ghia's job was simply to get them built. A long line of Chrysler specials with bodies made in Italy began with the K-310 of 1952.

The letter K stood for Keller, and it was said that the number 310 stood for horsepower, but the engine was in fact a stock Saratoga V-8 rated at 180 SAE gross hp. Described as "entirely new, with a European flavor," the K-310 was a bulbous two-seater coupe with a bold eggcrate grille and clean flanks. To break up the slab sides, Exner designed a "hitch" into the side skin and insisted on full fender cutouts for the wheels. "The wheel is one of man's oldest and most vital inventions," he said. "Why attempt to hide it?"

Next in Exner's show-car program came two Styling Specials, appropriately named "SS" by the designers. The first one, a fastback coupe, was built on a shortened New Yorker chassis with 119-inch wheelbase, and the second, a notchback coupe, had a stock chassis about six inches longer. Both were powered by stock Chrysler V-8 engines.

"These two cars were designed in Dad's basement in Birmingham [Michigan]," said Virgil Exner, Jr. "They were done as quarter-scale models, whereas the K-310 had been a three-eighths."

The building of the SS prototypes was not sponsored by the Chrysler Corporation, but privately by C. B. Thomas. The long-wheelbase notchback was his personal car, and its roofline is closely suggestive of the design for the VW Karmann-Ghia coupe.

A special case can be made for the Chrysler D'elegance (factory spelling) as the direct progenitor of the VW Karmann-Ghia. Drawings and a clay model from Chrysler were sent to Ghia, and the finished product appeared early in 1953, on a 115-inch wheelbase, powered by a stock Chrysler V-8 engine. There were points of resemblance. Though the D'elegance was a fastback, its greenhouse had something of the Karmann-Ghia's airiness about it. It had almost the same crease line in the side skin, linking the horizontal doorsill with the rear fender edges.

Virgil Exner offered this explanation: "I had the D'elegance being built over in Turin. Of course, we had prepared a very detailed plaster model for them to work from. At the same time, they were working on prototypes for VW, for what became the Karmann-Ghia. They had done two or three, and Karmann was still not satisfied. This plaster model of mine came in, and lo and behold, when the Karmann-Ghia came out, it was scaled right down to the fraction."

This statement is supported by his son, in no uncertain terms: "The D'elegance was just dead nuts on the whole Karmann-Ghia idea, except that on account of the rear engine, the nose was changed. I went to school for a time in Austria, and saw the prototype down in Turin. They asked my opinion: 'Did it look too much like the D'elegance?' I said, 'Hell, no—it looked *just* like it.'"

Eager to expand its manufacturing side, Ghia asked for and received Chrysler's permission to produce and market the D'elegance coupe in limited numbers. It evolved into a new model called the GS-1, and about 400 such cars were built. Most of them were sold through Société France Motors of Paris, the French importer and distributor for Chrysler.

The Turin-Osnabrück-Wolfsburg triangle.

In Europe today, nobody is alive to claim credit for the design of the VW Karmann-Ghia coupe. But the idea that it was an Exner design had not occurred to those who were associated with the project or part of the three-way partnership.

I went to Volkswagen's archives, where the critical years, 1950-55, were blank in terms of shedding light on the start of the project. While visiting Karmann in Osnabrück, I got an interview with the owner, Dr. Wilhelm Karmann, Jr., son of the founder.

Could he recall what went on? He agreed to reveal all he knew: "In the years 1950-51-52 I had numerous discussions with Volkswagen executives in Wolfsburg on the subject of a sports convertible using the Beetle chassis. We were, of course, producing the four-seater convertible at the time, using the main body panels of the Beetle. This was talked about as something quite different, more in the way of a roadster."

His opening statement is important in several ways. It gives certain chronological hinges for further debate, in that it fixes the year of the start of negotiations for a production model involving Karmann as 1950. Moreover, it makes it clear that the project was still in the planning stage as late as 1952. As for defining the type of vehicle, the concept seems vague, and the term roadster does not apply to any production version of the VW Karmann-Ghias that stemmed from these discussions.

"These discussions," continued Dr. Karmann, "were followed by frequent conversations with Dr. Feuereisen, vice president of Volkswagen and responsible for sales, and also with Ludwig Boehner, the engineer who was then director of product development at Wolfsburg. We had some ideas about what such a car might look like, and we made several small-scale models with our own styling concepts here at Osnabrück. These were duly submitted to the Volkswagen management. But the word came back to us that they were not quite satisfied with any of the models we had made.

"I must say that due to the Volkswagen's chassis configuration and dimensions, it was a very difficult job to create a good-looking sports-car body for it."

From what Dr. Karmann told me, it is clear that it was the stylists and designers on Karmann's staff who were assigned to this not-so-easy task. In other words, as far as Karmann was concerned, Carrozzeria Ghia was not involved at this stage. How did the link between Karmann and Ghia come into existence?

Dr. Karmann readily explained: "Over the years, with many visits to auto shows in Turin, Paris, Geneva and so on, I had become acquainted with Luigi Segre. He was owner and president of Carrozzeria Ghia, and we became good friends. One day I explained to him my thoughts about the Volkswagen sports car, and asked him to make a prototype.

Wilhelm Karmann, Jr., at the wheel of a VW Golf convertible. Before the Ghia designs came to be, Volkswagen's brass had rejected several sports-coupe proposals by Karmann's artists.

"He did not immediately say, 'Yes, I will do that.' When we parted, he had not actually promised to do anything. But I could see that he was intrigued with the idea, and I knew he would give it careful consideration."

There is no contradiction or conflict in these statements with the allegations that Exner designed the Karmann-Ghia. It is made clear that Karmann did not seek out Ghia's help because it needed help with prototype construction, but strictly because it needed to go outside for styling inspiration. And it is understood that neither Karmann nor Volkswagen had any sort of a target date for production. The fate of the project was totally contingent upon coming up with a prototype that would get Volkswagen's approval.

One would guess that once Luigi Segre entered the picture, the story would shift into overdrive. But that's not the case, according to Dr. Karmann: "Without informing us or telling the Volkswagen management, Segre then went to Paris to see a mutual friend of ours, Charles Ladouche, who was then the French importer of Volkswagen and Chrysler cars. Segre talked Ladouche into supplying him with a standard VW Beetle. The car was brought to the Ghia works in Turin, where it was rebuilt according to the designs which Segre had prepared in the meantime.

"When I made a trip to Paris later in the year, 1953, Segre and Ladouche had a great surprise waiting for me in the shape of this prototype. It was a coupe—not a convertible. Before the end of the year I arranged to present it to Dr. Feuereisen. His reaction was immediate: 'Now that has Class!'"

This statement is highly relevant, mainly for fixing certain events on the calendar. It establishes the fact that Ghia had completed the D'elegance before showing the VW prototype to Dr. Karmann, and was in full swing building the 400 GS-1 coupes, for which Charles Ladouche (as owner of Société France Motors) took care of marketing.

"Up to that time," Dr. Karmann continued, "nobody here in Osnabrück knew anything about the project. My engineers saw it first as a model on a one-to-one scale. After their first astonishment, we began to examine the model and talk about the problems of building it. It could not use the standard frame or platform of the Beetle. That was the main thing about it. The Beetle has this central tube, with a platform on each side. On this frame, they put the body-in-white [raw, complete body shell before treatment and painting], and bolted the whole thing together. We had to change this.

"We kept the front suspension and steering, the rear end with engine and transmission, and the central tube with the gearshift and other controls. But we had to build an entirely new floor structure, 118 mm wider than the standard one, with its own doorsills and other reinforcements.

"While the reengineering of the chassis was being done on the drawing board, we invited Heinz Nordhoff to come and see the prototype. He looked it over from all sides, taking a long time to examine it in detail. Finally he said to me, 'I must admit that it is a very beautiful car, but much too expensive.' 'How can you say that?' I retorted, 'when I have not even told you what it costs!'"

The rest was business, far divorced from styling concepts and design work, as Dr. Karmann recounts: "Then I laid down our conditions, and Nordhoff soon realized that it was indeed possible to build this car and sell it at a reasonable, competitive price. The contract was duly signed. Volkswagenwerk would supply us with the Export-model Beetle chassis, and we would produce the bodies, complete with interiors, and assemble the car. We were to deliver the final product to the Volkswagen sales organization, which would be in charge of distribution."

Wilhelm Karmann, Jr., was born on December 4, 1914. He went to school in Osnabrück and at the age of nineteen went to work in the parental establishment. He completed his training period, including a stint with a well-known coachbuilder in south Germany, and returned to Westfalen.

From 1935 to 1937 he attended the Institute for Coachwork and Vehicle Construction at Bernau near Berlin, and followed that up with two years as an engineer with Ambi-Budd in Berlin, the local subsidiary of the Edward G. Budd Company that had pioneered the all-steel body, the unit-construction body, and was producing bodies for a number of German car companies as well as issuing licenses to others.

Thus Wilhelm Karmann quickly became familiar with the most advanced techniques in body engineering and manufacturing. Returning to Osnabrück in 1939, he took charge of converting the production to military-equipment orders before he became a soldier in 1941. He was taken prisoner by the Americans and returned to Osnabrück at the end of 1945.

Sergio Coggiola, who worked on the first Karmann-Ghia prototype and later became Ghia's chief engineer for Karmann products, now has his own establishment at Orbassano.

After his father's death at the age of eighty-eight in 1952, Wilhelm Karmann, Jr., became majority shareholder and chief executive officer of the company that bears his name. All his statements must be taken in good faith, including the account of the surprising maneuvers that kept him from knowing how the car was designed.

Having exhausted German sources, I went to Turin for a series of interviews with Italians. One of the first to speak out was Sergio Coggiola, owner and president of his own styling studio and prototype construction shops at Orbassano. He remembers doing detail drawings for the VW in 1953, having joined Ghia in 1952 as a body engineer. "The overall design was done by Boano," he said.

But Coggiola had no idea as to whether Boano had been influenced, and to what extent, by Exner's Chrysler designs. Could no one confirm that it was in fact an adaptation from an American design, suitably and selectively scaled down or, alternatively, dig up any evidence that the Karmann-Ghia shape existed prior to Ghia's work for Chrysler? I spent a lot of hours asking questions of people who were active in positions of responsibility in the Italian auto industry in the early fifties.

For a long time, I failed to reach anyone who claimed inside knowledge of Ghia's operations and transactions at the time. Then suddenly that changed: "My father prepared the basic designs for the VW coupe in 1950." With those simple words, Gian Paolo Boano made his bid to set the record straight.

The son of Mario Boano, who was twenty-five years of age when the Karmann-Ghia went into production, was assisting his father throughout the critical period of 1950-55, and retains a clear memory of the main events and their sequence. Gian Paolo Boano is now head of Fiat's styling center in Turin, having worked in car design and construction all his life.

His statements are in open opposition to those of the Exners, father and son, and we must again prepare to engage in a little historical analysis, balancing fresh testimony against known facts.

Mario Felice Boano was born in Turin in 1903 and graduated from the San Carlo Technical College. His first job was with Stabilimenti Farina, coachbuilders, aircraft engine manufacturers and pioneers of hydraulic shock absorbers, power-top convertibles and other automotive devices.

In 1930, when Pinin Farina left the family establishment to set up his own shop, Boano joined the younger of the Farina brothers. He left to start his own business about 1935 and worked under contract with several coachbuilding firms to produce designs, wooden models and so on.

In 1946 he merged his enterprise with Carrozzeria Ghia, whose founder, Giacinto Ghia, had died in 1944. And by 1948, the Ghia family had sold out in full to Boano.

Known as a craftsman rather than as an artist, many of Boano's postwar creations for Ghia had a ponderous look, and he seemed unable to break loose from prewar concepts and proportions, until 1949 when he entered a period of striking originality and prolific creativity. His grilleless, round-front Alfa Romeo 6C 2500 S convertible was exhibited in 1949, and a version of the Karmann-Ghia rear-fender treatment (with leading

Porsche Type 64 streamlined coupe, built in 1938 for the proposed Berlin-Rome road race, had a Volkswagen chassis. It can be claimed to be the direct forerunner of the Karmann-Ghia coupe.

edge extending from a horizontal crease line through the doors) was first used on a Lancia Aurelia limousine in 1950. We also find the beginnings of the VW coupe greenhouse on Ghia's Gioiello coupe on Fiat 1100 chassis in 1949.

Thus it is established that some of the main styling elements of the Karmann-Ghia had been realized not only on paper but in hard metal in 1949-50, and there is no reason to disbelieve Gian Paolo Boano when he says that the basic design for the VW coupe was done a whole year or more before Luigi Segre initiated the cooperation with Chrysler. But why wasn't the prototype built until 1953? Or, looking at it from the opposite end, why was Boano interested in the VW as a basis for a sports coupe as early as 1950?

Frontal aspect of the Porsche Type 64 Berlin-Rome prototype shows no Italian styling influence at all, but was based strictly on aerodynamic studies in German wind tunnels.

To discuss the second question first, Boano wasn't the only one who had the idea of using the VW chassis as a basis for a sports car. Porsche was certainly the first, with the Type 64 of 1938. It was a streamlined coupe with body by Rupflin of Munich, built specifically for the proposed Berlin-Rome (Axis Power) road race that never took place. It can be regarded as a direct forerunner of the Porsche Type 356, about fifty of which were built in Austria in 1948-49, using Volkswagen chassis. Wolfgang Denzel produced a number of VW-based sports cars in Vienna from 1948 to 1960, and Friedrich Rometsch built sports car bodies for the VW chassis in Berlin from 1949 to 1961.

The fact that Ghia was an Italian firm, while the others were located in Germany and Austria, only attests to Boano's international orien-

The Porsche Type 64 has been preserved and is part of the Porsche collection. The photos were taken at the Nürburgring in 1982. The roadsters in the background are DKW (left) and Skoda (right), with the tail end of a Lancia Aurelia B-20 coupe.

tation. Ghia had in fact been working for Renault of France even earlier, as a consultant for the body design of the big Fregate that went into production in 1951.

As for Ghia's lateness in finishing the VW prototype, it is not difficult to explain. As we know from Wilhelm Karmann, Jr., there was no contact between Ghia and Karmann in 1950. Luigi Segre did not join Ghia until the end of 1950. And Gian Paolo Boano explained: "This VW-based design was my father's idea. But when he tried to get delivery of a Beetle chassis from Volkswagen, they refused."

The story might have ended right there had it not been for a similar idea being born to Karmann, and Segre's superb olfactory sense for finding out where he could make a deal.

It now transpires, however, that the VW coupe design was not done "in the meantime," as Karmann thought, but had been ready before the

The first car to bear the name Porsche was built in Austria in 1948, using a Volkswagen chassis. It provided inspiration for Denzel and Rometsch, and influenced Ghia's thinking to include the VW.

Westfalian first talked to Segre about the project. Dr. Karmann had been thinking in terms of "something more in the way of a roadster" but Ghia's existing design was a two-seater coupe.

Karmann's statements also make nonsense of Exner's remark that Karmann had turned down two or three proposed Ghia designs, for nothing was shown to Karmann until he went to Paris where Segre and Ladouche put the finished car before him. On the other hand, Volkswagen had rejected some earlier designs by Karmann, which Segre had probably become aware of, and may have told Exner about. If that is what Exner meant to refer to, it becomes only a matter of a slight misunderstanding or disremembering.

Reflecting further upon the similarity of certain Chrysler show cars to the VW coupe, one fact stands out: The Chrysler cars were built by Ghia. Period. Inevitably some Ghia influence could show up in the Chrysler cars, simply due to the construction methods and individual habits of the craftsmen. And no doubt certain liberties were taken, deliberately or subconsciously, with the Chrysler scale models and drawings sent over from Detroit.

Most of this influence would have been in invisible detail, but it is a plausible theory that Ghia's artists might have tried to "improve" on some

The Porsche roadster was given the number 356 and served as a basis for Porsche's regular production models for almost 20 years. Indirectly it was also an ancestor of the Karmann-Ghia.

of Exner's work. That would explain, for instance, how the open-duct air intakes with the prominent horizontal brows, flanking the vertical Alfa Romeo grille on a 1900-C coupe by Ghia in 1952, could find their way to the front end of the Chrysler D'elegance in 1953.

The point I want to make with these speculations is to suggest that, in cases of similarities between Ghia-built Chrysler cars and Ghia designs for other clients, the flow of styling influence ran counter to the direction claimed by the Exners. In other words, not from Chrysler to Ghia, but just the reverse. When I asked Gian Paolo Boano whether he agreed with this conclusion he answered, "Yes, yes, that should be obvious."

Gian Paolo Boano also confirmed Karmann's story that the chassis for the prototype coupe was in fact a complete Beetle, supplied to Ghia by Charles Ladouche. "I went to Paris to fetch it," he recalled, "and had trouble with the customs at the Franco-Italian border because I had no import license for the car."

That must have been in March or April 1953, for Gian Paolo Boano is positive on the point that the complete prototype was built in five months from the date of the Beetle's arrival in Turin. It was in August or September that Dr. Karmann saw it in Paris. From there, the car went back to the Ghia factory in Turin, presumably for some more work to be done on it. "We sold the car to Karmann," said Gian Paolo Boano, "and shipped it in an armored truck to Osnabrück.

Dr. Karmann confirmed both the purchase and the secrecy that surrounded the transaction. "No one in Osnabrück was informed of the project. I had cleared out some space in Hall One of the plant, and put up big curtains. Then the Ghia prototype was brought inside one dark night." Why all this mystery? For two reasons, the first being social and the second political. Dr. Karmann did not want his staff and workers to feel the excitement and build up their hopes only to suffer disappointment in case Volkswagen did not sign an agreement for going into production.

The political considerations were more compelling, for Dr. Karmann feared the VW contract could be jeopardized unless he was able to give full assurance to the men of Wolfsburg that no one other than himself, Ladouche and the Ghia personnel involved had seen the car or knew that it was now Karmann's property.

Then followed a period of manufacturing studies and calculations to get an idea of what it would cost to build.

On November 16, 1953, Dr. Nordhoff and Dr. Feuereisen went to Osnabrück at Dr. Karmann's invitation to see the car. Both were highly impressed, and since Nordhoff was a man of both impulse and determination, it was concluded right away that it was going to be built.

A period of intimate collaboration between the Karmann engineers and the body and chassis experts of Wolfsburg was to follow.

"We were able to build the restyled car only because we engineered a new, wider floor," explained Dr. Karmann. "Ghia did just the original styling prototype. We had to build the test cars here in our own shop."

Several disguised prototypes were made for on-the-road testing, and they covered hundreds of thousands of kilometers before the structure was cleared for production.

"How many test cars did we have?" Dr. Karmann repeated my question to himself, and went on: "Not many. Nowadays, the car companies build maybe fifty or eighty prototypes that are tested before the design is frozen and production tooling ordered. But in those days, if you had two, three or four test cars, you felt like a large-scale manufacturer. We had four or five test cars. That's all. Test cars are very expensive, and we could not afford more."

Hermann Kriegenherdt was Karmann's chief engineer on the VW coupe project, and two of the men on his team, Gottfried Niemann and Gerd Gieseke, are still with Karmann today. Niemann explained: "We had to change the chassis to fit the body, and we did this by widening the side panels in the platform frame by about 80 mm on each side. In collaboration with our colleagues at Volkswagen, we lowered the springs and changed the shock absorbers. Also, the steering column was tilted downwards, and the gearshift lever was shortened." The tooling costs ran into millions of D-Marks.

Detailed drawings of several hundred new parts had to be made up and production arranged. At this time they were thinking in terms of 250 to 400 bodies a month, since no one had a precise idea of how this car would sell.

It took Karmann less than eighteen months to get ready for production, from the moment the prototype arrived at Osnabrück.

Segre, Ladouche and Karmann wanted to display the prototype at the Paris Salon in October 1954, but Feuereisen managed to block that plan. Karl Feuereisen had been Auto Union's racing manager before the war, and held considerable authority in the VW organization. He did not want anything to be shown that was not for sale. And most of the men involved had to agree, years later, that his tactics were right. Regrettably, he died in June 1955, just as the sports coupe was going into production.

In the spring of 1955 Karmann had 1,770 people working in the plant, of which over 1,000 were in the body shops. Karmann was then building the last of the DKW convertibles, after a run of 6,500 four-seaters and 420 sports roadsters. A little later, in July 1955, production of the Ford Taunus Kombi came to an end. Over 9,000 had been made. Production of the VW coupe got under way in June, slowly at first, then gradually speeding up.

Initially, the launching of the car was set for August 27, 1955, a couple of weeks before the opening of the Frankfurt auto show (September 19, 1955). But the problem of finding a place to store the finished cars in June, July and most of August dictated an earlier release date. Dr. Wilhelm Karmann convinced Nordhoff that the car should be introduced on July 14, France's Bastille Day, perhaps in recognition of Charles Ladouche's vital part in making the whole scheme possible. The press presentation was arranged at the Kasino Hotel of Georgsmarienhütte in Westfalen, a few miles south of Osnabrück.

It was a world sensation," recalled Dr. Karmann, "but it still did not have a name. I had been discussing the question of naming it with Dr. Feuereisen and Heinz Nordhoff. To capitalize on the Italian-styled body, we thought of names like Ascona, San Remo, Corona and other lake, mountain or seaside resorts. Some we rejected right away, others we considered possible. But time was getting short. The car was going on sale in October, and we needed a marketing name, a trademark, before that. Finally I said: 'How about calling it the Karmann-Ghia?' They looked at me, tried it out on their lips as if to taste it, and decided they liked it. Everybody was in favor of the Karmann-Ghia name. And so it was sold as the Volkswagen Karmann-Ghia. It did a lot of good for Ghia, for their design got the recognition it deserved."

Chapter Three

THE CAREER OF THE KARMANN-GHIA

While Nordhoff was in charge of Volkswagen, the financial press on repeated occasions, particularly in his last years, took him to task for what they called his "monoculture," meaning a one-model policy. That was largely a myth. With his GM experience, Nordhoff had a marvelous comprehension of how to juggle model variations, rationalized componentry, production costs and market appeal.

He also understood better than anyone that Volkswagen was not General Motors. It wasn't even a German counterpart to Chevrolet. It was a mass producer of ordinary cars for the people. As the industries of other European countries recovered from the war, Volkswagen found that Renault, Citroen, Fiat, Austin, Morris, Ford and Standard were out to compete for the very same customers.

Nordhoff looked at their products, some of which were conventional, others even more radical in their technical concepts, and determined that the Volkswagen formula was sound. The emphasis was not to be placed on model changes, but on quality, dependability, long life, simplified maintenance schedule, reasonably priced spare parts and competent service personnel—on a worldwide basis.

As for the one-model policy, it was an empty accusation. In fact, Nordhoff did everything he could to broaden the product range. He came to Wolfsburg at the start of 1948. Within two years, he had the van (Transporter/Microbus) in production. That's not a one-model policy. But the van (Type 2) did share the Beetle (Type 1) chassis, his detractors assert. Production engineers everywhere, faced with the economic realities of carmaking on a daily basis, would say that's only intelligent sharing of components. The worst that Nordhoff can be accused of is a one-family policy, and there were several contemporary auto companies who wished they could come up with a diversified product range where all models belonged in the same family.

No sooner was Type 2 on the market than Nordhoff was ready to discuss further broadening of the model range with Wilhelm Karmann, Jr. Nordhoff's conditions were that new models must be part of the same family, must not run into uncontrollable production cost, and must find a ready, stable and international market.

He didn't hesitate to give the green light for the Karmann-Ghia when he saw that it met his conditions. Nordhoff also understood that a constant effort in the area of product development was necessary to keep up with the competition and maintain viability in the market place. This insight was paired with an almost perverse will to delay improvements (such as a fuel gauge, synchromesh transmission and an effective heater) so long that the VW reputation could have suffered and certain market segments become alienated from VW. In contrast, he seemed almost rash in his readiness to commit huge funds to retooling with more modern machinery and equipment, for building cars that were described—with growing frequency —as obsolescent or obsolete.

The VW chassis was designed at the outset of the Autobahn era, with the unique feature that the engine was always under-stressed, and its top speed was also a safe cruising speed. But the front and rear suspension systems were designed with an incomplete understanding of roll centers and vehicle dynamics. And the rearward bias in weight distribution, which was excellent for traction under low-friction road conditions, negated whatever ambitions Prof. Porsche may have had with regard to roadholding and directional stability.

The Karmann-Ghia chassis.

From an industrial viewpoint, everything argued in favor of keeping the Beetle's exact same engine and drive train—in fact, the majority of all mechanical parts—for the Karmann-Ghia.

Though often referred to as a "platform" frame, the VW frame was really a central tube "backbone" frame with a forked rear end. The platform was a two-piece structure, welded to the tube, with integral cross-members for structural strength.

For the Karmann-Ghia, the basic platform was altered to permit the fitting of a wider body. For instance, the main carrying side-members were moved farther apart so as to permit the use of the same parts as much as possible. A tubular, 12-mm-diameter stabilizer bar was added to the front suspension, anchored in rubber bushings, crossing the chassis in front of the lower cross-member, and linking the two lower trailing arms.

The engine and transmission were taken unchanged from the Export-model Beetle. This engine, including clutch and exhaust system, cooling fan and ducting, weighed 90 kg (198.5 pounds) and was carried in the rear overhang, behind the final drive unit.

Some chassis modifications were necessary to get the engine to fit under the lower deck of the sports coupe. The solution was to use the suspended air filter and angled duct from the Type 2 Volkswagen. That meant revising the carburetor jetting accordingly, with a 180 compensating jet instead of the Beetle's 195 jet.

It was quite deliberate on Volkswagen's part that the Karmann-Ghia did not possess more power and performance. Neither Nordhoff nor Feue-

Cross-section of the 1192 cc Volkswagen engine. Because of the cooling-fan mounting, the very flat unit turned into a rather tall installation package.

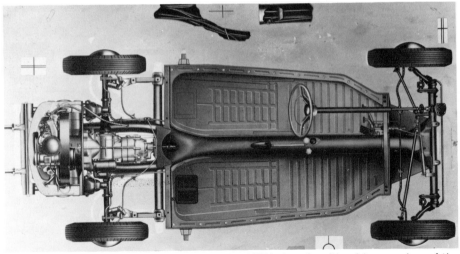

The Karmann-Ghia was built on a standard VW chassis with wider spacing of the side rails. This is a 1958 version, with the new gas pedal and dished steering wheel.

reisen wanted to risk seeing their pretty doll made to look ridiculous on the racetrack. Consequently there was no thought of getting Porsche to develop a higher-powered engine for it, nor to offer an optional supercharger.

In 1948 Dr. Nordhoff had signed an exclusive agreement with the Porsche company, securing for Volkswagen a top-priority claim on Porsche's engineering capacity, while committing VW not to go elsewhere for any technical assistance on the product front.

In fact, tuning the Volkswagen engine was a difficult thing, to the great puzzlement of tuning experts who were used to water-cooled engines only. Overheating problems would set in if the compression ratio was substantially raised. All it could take without trouble was a dual-carburetor setup or a low-pressure supercharger. Such conversions became quite popular for the Beetle in the German, British and American aftermarket.

One of the first on the market was the Okrasa tuning kit, with special cylinder heads, camming, valves, valve springs, porting and manifold headers. Soon afterward, the Swiss firm M.A.G. was out with a low-pressure Roots-type supercharger. In America it was the Roots-type Pepco and the

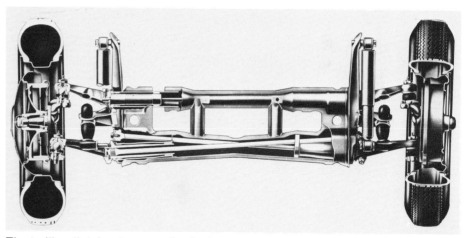

The trailing-link front suspension had torsion bars that crossed each other between the lower links. Shock absorbers were mounted vertically at the inboard pivot points.

vane-type Judson superchargers that became most popular. They have probably contributed to the decision-making underlying the successive enlargements of the VW engine.

The Karmann body.

What Karmann received from Ghia was a prototype car, handmade by skilled craftsmen, and a set of two-dimensional drawings. Karmann's

First production-model Karmann-Ghia coupe shows high fidelity to Ghia's design details. This car is now part of the Karmann collection.

Ghia prototype was accurately followed in terms of sheet metal, but the production model was to differ in detail. Most obvious difference was the missing "nostrils."

Rear end of the Ghia prototype was faithfully followed by Karmann engineers down to detail designs, including brightwork, vents and lights. But the Ghia bumper was redesigned.

engineers had to translate everything from styling lingo to production terms, which meant going over everything with manufacturing needs and possibilities in mind.

The body was welded together from sheet-metal stampings into a complete shell according to the best unit-construction methods, but the shell was practically free from stress-bearing duties. All normal load and bending forces were calculated to be handled by the platform frame. The body shell was *bolted* to the platform.

Since Karmann had no really big presses at the time, the sizes of the individual body shell pressings were quite small. The front end was made of five separate pieces, with weld joints running in some of the most unlikely places. In contrast with the Beetle body, the coupe fenders were not removable, but welded into the body shell as integral parts of the structure. There were 3.5 meters (nearly 140 inches) of welds on the outer skin,

First production model differed from the prototype in having "nostril" type vents, curved side glass and wider chrome strips around the windows.

and the stampings were water-cooled in the assembly jig to keep them from distorting.

Several innovations usually seen only on one-off show cars or very expensive custom-built bodies were included in the production-model specifications.

The doors did not extend above the belt line and had frameless door glass. The window glass had a slight inward curve toward the top, and the door opening was one meter wide to permit easy entry and exit.

Not common in those days, the use of curved glass all around was part of the Ghia formula. Door handles were of the fixed type, with push-button lock releases. The doors were hinged at the front edge, a natural for safety, at a time when a number of French and British cars still featured bodies with rear-hinged "suicide" doors that opened at the forward edge.

Both the "hood" ahead of the windshield and the engine cover (rear deck lid) had spring-loaded "over-center" hinges to keep the lids in open position without the use of stays or rods. On the rear deck were four rows of louvers, neatly grouped along the forward edge (above the fan shrouding).

Chrome strips ran from fender opening to fender opening on each side. The bumpers, headlight surrounds, blinker frames, reversing light and license plate light, door handles, hubcaps and rim embellishers were chrome-plated.

A second version of the two-plus-two coupe by Ghia had a wraparound rear window, as often used on Ghia bodies for other clients.

As early as 1954, Ghia proposed a two-plus-two version of the VW coupe. Ghia built a prototype to order by Karmann, but Volkswagen turned it down.

The locks for the front and rear lids were operated via bowden cable from pull-buttons operated by the driver. The front "hood" button was located under the instrument panel on the left side, and the engine cover release button was placed just inside the doorsill, on the back seat base.

The "trunk" between the front wheels was in fact roomier than on the Beetle, and could hold 200 liters (seven cubic feet). It was 1,250 mm (49.2 inches) wide, 340 mm (13.4 inches) high and 470 mm (18.5 inches) long. To make this possible, the coupe had a special low-profile fuel tank, with forty-liter (10.5-gallon) capacity, which had an additional benefit in lowering the center of gravity.

Karmann built its first convertible back in 1954, in the days before the "nostrils" had been drawn into the frontal aspect.

Also, the coupe differed from the Beetle in carrying the battery back in the engine compartment, instead of up front. It was a 6-volt, 66-amp-hour battery of the same type.

The overall styling impression was right for its time—not ahead, nor behind. Today, we would question the high belt line, the drooping tail and the bulbous nose, but never the overall proportions.

Behind the emergency seat backrest was an empty space reserved for luggage, accessible only from inside the car. It could hold 160 liters (5.65 cubic feet) being 570 mm (22.4 inches) in length, 940 mm (37 inches) in width and 340 mm (13.4 inches) in height. Access was gained by swinging the backrest forward and down. Leaving it folded would almost double the luggage capacity.

The windshield angle was about fifty degrees, and the glass had a maximum width of 1,200 mm (47.2 inches) and a maximum height of 425 mm (16.7 inches) measured along the surface. It was gently curved to the sides with a near-constant radius. The rear window also had curved glass and was inclined at an angle of about sixty degrees. Its maximum width was 1,100 mm (43.3 inches) and its greatest height was 430 mm (16.9 inches) measured along the surface.

Since the Karmann-Ghia coupe was intended as a civilized touring car, passenger comfort was an objective that came in for close attention and much effort.

Karmann-Ghia 1955 model in profile. Instead of a Ghia badge on the left fender skirt, the production car carried a Karmann emblem on the right one.

The front seats were wide and well padded, and the extra seat in the back had a thick foam rubber cushion. The reclining seats were adjustable for height as well as fore-and-aft, and the backrests folded forward to allow access to the space behind. The coupe had a hip room dimension of 1,380 mm (54.3 inches) compared with 1,230 mm (48.4 inches) for the Beetle sedan.

Vinyl upholstery was optional, cloth standard. Rubber mats on the floor were standard, and the luggage spaces were carpeted.

The heating system, naturally, was adapted from the Beetle sedan, and consequently had the same drawbacks. The biggest disadvantage was that the heating air was slow to warm up, and under many conditions never got warm enough. This is an inherent problem with air-cooled engines. In this system, hot air was drawn from the engine-cooling airflow, and admitted through outlets at foot level and on top of the instrument panel for windshield demisting. A twist-button for temperature control was mounted

Controls and instrument panel of the 1955-model Karmann-Ghia. The Beetle's utter simplicity had been conserved, even with a lid on the glovebox.

on the floor tunnel, mixing heated and unheated air in the theoretically desired quantities.

The speedometer read to 140 km/h (87 mph) and was accompanied by a big clock on its right. Both dials had a 110 mm (4.33 inch) diameter. The wiper switch and the light switch were located on the right, next to the clock, while the ignition lock and starter button were mounted adjacent to the speedometer on the left. Wiper motors were standard Beetle-type, but the wiper arms, blades and linkage were new.

In the middle of the instrument panel, there was space for a radio and speaker. The dome light was moved to the top of the windshield, and the rear fenders had a combined lens for brake, reversing and turn indicator lights.

The prototype had a split bumper, parking lights inboard of the headlamps, at a lower level, and prominent Ghia emblems on the fender skirts. For the production model, the parking lights were placed directly below the headlamps, and both front and rear bumpers were of the full width type, with central license plate mountings, flanked by overrider bars.

The amount of luggage space available in the Karmann-Ghia was amazing. The secret was the extra compartment above the transmission.

SPECIFICATIONS
Volkswagen two-seater coupe "Karmann-Ghia" Type 143 and Type 144
Valid as of March 26, 1955

Architecture
Rear-mounted engine, rear-wheel drive. Fuel tank and spare wheel between front wheels. Luggage space between front wheels and behind seats.

Dimensions
Wheelbase	2400 mm	94.5 in.
Track, front	1290 mm	51.0 in.
Track, rear	1250 mm	49.2 in.
Overall length	4140 mm	163.0 in.
Overall width	1630 mm	64.2 in.
Overall height (unladen)	1325 mm	52.2 in.
Ground clearance	172 mm	6.8 in.
Minimum turn diameter	11.25 m	36.9 ft.

Weight
Dry weight	790 kg	1742 lb.
Payload capacity	300 kg	661.5 lb.
Maximum all-up weight	1110 kg	2448 lb.
Maximum front end load	450 kg	992 lb.
Maximum rear end load	660 kg	1455 lb.

Engine
Layout	Horizontally opposed 4-cylinder with individual finned cylinders screwed into a common crankcase.
Cooling	Forced air: radial fan mounted on a horizontal shaft shared with the generator, and driven by V-belt from a crankshaft pulley. Automatic airflow control by thermostat in blower entry duct.
Bore	77 mm — 3.03 in.
Stroke	64 mm — 2.52 in.
Displacement	1192 cc — 72.7 cu. in.
Compression ratio	6.6:1
Carburetor	1 Solex downdraft 28 PCI with acceleration pump and cold-starting device.
Valves	Overhead, in line with cylinder axis, operated by pushrods and rocker arms.
Valve timing	Inlet opens 2.5° BTC
	Inlet closes 37.5° ABC
	Exhaust opens 37.5° BBC
	Exhaust closes 2.5° ATC
Camshaft	Cast iron with integral cams. Base circle, 24.5 mm, 0.96 in.; lift, 7.45 mm, 0.29 in. Located directly below the crankshaft and driven by spur gears.
Crankshaft	One-plane forged steel, counterweighted, running in four main bearings.
Connecting rods	I-profile, forged steel, 130 mm (5.12 in.) center-to-center.
Pistons	Cast aluminum with steel insert
Output	30 hp DIN @ 3400 rpm, 36 hp SAE gross @ 3600 rpm
Torque	7.7 m-kg @ 2000 rpm, 64 lb. ft. @ 2400 rpm

Drive train
Clutch	Single dry plate
Transmission	4-speed manual gearbox, synchromesh on second, third and fourth.
Gear ratios	1st, 3.60:1; 2nd, 1.88; 3rd, 1.23; 4th, 0.82; Rev, 4.53.
Final drive	Spiral bevel
Final drive ratio	4.43:1

Chassis
Front suspension	Dual trailing links per wheel (upper and lower), with transverse laminated torsion bars and double-acting telescopic shock absorbers. Stabilizer bar, adding 10 m-kg per degree to roll stiffness.	
Rear suspension	Pendulum-type swing axles with trailing arms, transverse torsion bars and double-acting telescopic shock absorbers.	
Front wheel rate	16 kg/cm	89.6 lb. per in.
Rear wheel rate	20 kg/cm	112 lb. per in.
Natural frequency under full load (cycles per minute)	83 front	77 rear
Steering	Worm-and-nut, with split track rod	
Steering gear ratio	14.15:1	

Overall steering ratio	17.6:1		Wheels and tires	Tire size 5.60 x 15
Turns, lock-to-lock	2.4			Rim size 4J-15
Maximum steering angle	26° (outside wheel), 32° (inside wheel)		Dynamic roll radius	307 mm 12.08 in.
			Inflation pressure	1.2 Bar (front) 18 psi
Steering wheel diameter	400 mm 15.75 in.			1.7 Bar (rear) 25 psi
Brakes	Hydraulic Ate-Simplex four-wheel brake system, duo-servo shoes, manual adjustment. Cast iron drums front and rear, no power assist. Mechanical handbrake acting on rear wheel drums.		*Performance*	
			Top speed	116 km/h 72 mph
			Acceleration	0-50 km/h (31 mph) 7.2 sec.
				0-60 km/h (37 mph) 10.8 sec.
				0-80 km/h (50 mph) 18.2 sec.
				0-100 km/h (62 mph) 31.5 sec.
			Fuel consumption	6.5 to 9.8 liters per 100 km (24 to 36 mpg)
Drum diameter	230 mm 9.06 in.			
Lining width	30 mm 1.18 in.		Hill-climbing ability	1st gear, 30% gradient; 2nd,
Lining area	520 cm² 80.6 sq. in.			17%; 3rd, 8%; 4th, 4.5%.
Pedal arm ratio	210/30 mm 8.27/1.18 in.			

Driving the Karmann-Ghia.

"It's a lot like driving a Volkswagen," was the first reaction of a well-known European journalist. Since it shared so much with the Beetle, it is hard to see how it could be otherwise. "It sounds like a Volkswagen, goes like a Volkswagen and corners like a Volkswagen," remarked another colleague.

The body design usually received high praise, but there was also a general feeling that the car failed to live up to its image of performance, a promise held out by its body type and styling.

In Germany, the Karmann-Ghia was nicknamed Lieschen Müller's Sportwagen—sort of translatable into Li'l Liza Miller's sports car. One gets the vision of a naive young female, as devoid of driving skills as of powers of passing automotive-consumer judgment.

A Swedish journalist, recognizing the esthetic merit of the design but deploring its lack of performance, called it an "impotent Apollo." Funny thing is, Karmann-Ghia drivers *felt* their cars were peppier than the Beetle. Perhaps the low seating position and an acute awareness of the car's exterior styling and streamlined look did more to produce that feeling than any actual push in the back from stepping on the gas.

While it was heavier than the Beetle, it was geared for slightly higher top speed, to take advantage of its smaller frontal area and better aerodynamics. It was not wind-tunnel tested before going into production, and its aerodynamic drag coefficient is not known. I would estimate it as falling in the region of 0.45.

The lower body (and lower center of gravity) had little or no effect on the coupe's directional stability. Like the Beetle, it had a serious problem with sensitivity to sidewinds. A little wind tunnel work could have done a lot to improve that situation.

Wind tunnel testing would also have been helpful in connection with the ventilation system. The doors had no vent panes, and there was a terrible wind noise and draft if the door windows were cranked down a little. Rear side windows did open, however, just a crack, to permit evacuation of stale air from the interior, without the roar and draft of the door windows.

A further ventilation problem stemmed from the fact that the body had no cowl vent. There was, consequently, no fresh-air ventilation through the system. The heater system could only feed heated air.

Perhaps the strongest quality of the car was just that—quality. Mechanically it had all the soundness of the Beetle, with its built-in longevity. The body was as good as custom-built, the doors closing with that

Export-model coupe from 1956. It had stronger bumpers and different turn signals, parking lights, brake lights and wiring.

typical "thud" that mass-produced cars cannot imitate. The interior looked expensive, and good materials were used everywhere. Knobs, buttons, cranks and switches, everything worked with precision, and felt so solid one tended to assume they would keep on working forever.

I found the comfort of the wide seats, with their contoured cushions and driving position, fully satisfactory, despite a certain intrusion of the front wheel housings into the foot space. The pedals were well spaced, though many drivers found them mounted too high off the floor. The steering wheel was at the right height, at a fashionable sports-car angle. The pull-up hand-brake was ideally positioned between the seats, and the gear lever came conveniently to hand.

The seats had a fore-and-aft adjustment range of about 100 mm (four inches) and could be raised about 10 mm (0.4 inch) to help short drivers get a better view of the road. Still, many found it inadequate, with the high instrument panel preventing them from seeing a clear outline of the "hood"

The first convertible came to the U.S. in 1957, complete with reinforced front bumper. VW still had a 6-volt electrical system.

and fenders. Otherwise, the visibility was good. The pillars were slim and the glass area big for the period.

Under normal conditions, the Karmann-Ghia was made for effortless driving. Once you were rolling at 40-plus mph, it had good top-gear performance, and ran smoothly and pleasantly. But you had to understand that you could not expect it to do things you could not do with any other Volkswagen, in terms of passing and cornering.

With enterprising methods (mainly a lot of gear-shifting) you could manage creditable average speeds on ordinary highways. But on uphill gradients the Karmann-Ghia could not keep up with some of the humblest and most underpowered American family cars any better than the Beetle.

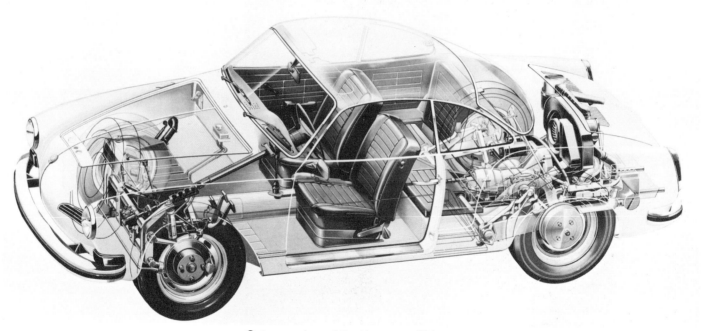

Cutaway view of the Karmann-Ghia coupe shows the disposition of the mechanical elements relative to seating. This is a post-1966 drawing (note disc brakes).

While the rear-mounted engine (and the large-diameter tires) gave it a big advantage in terms of traction on low-friction surfaces, such as ice, snow and mud, the rearward bias in weight distribution (not alleviated by the swing axles) could cause a frightening instability (oversteer), gaining momentum as if feeding on itself, so that any sideslip of the rear wheels brought with it a menace of losing control. In spite of the coupe's lower center of gravity, the suspension geometry had not been altered, with the result that the roadholding was just about the same as for the Beetle.

Rear view of the 1957-model convertible, showing repositioned louvers and a non-standard rear bumper.

Canopy for the soft-top Karmann-Ghia was a snug fit, made to keep rain out of the seats when the car was parked with the top down.

The steering was light and quick, which helped promote a feeling of sportiness among owners who had little or no experience driving real sports cars. The addition of a front stabilizer bar assured a certain speed-up of the steering response, which was a boon in difficult situations; for without rapid correction, the slightest tail slide on a wet corner (even at no more than 25 mph) would build up into an uncontrollable broadside and end in a spinout.

The safest cornering method was to enter a curve at reduced speed, then keep a steady foot on the accelerator and press down only when the next straight line was directly ahead.

Downshifting was advisable for any curve where lateral accelerations beyond 0.5 g could be expected, so as to have enough torque on tap to pull out of a tail-end skid. Though the engine did have a favorable torque curve, vigorous gear-shifting was advisable for safety on give-and-take roads.

In some respects, the gearbox was faultless. It was possible to make snappy shifts, but due to the long and vague linkage, a lack of precision was felt in every movement. Still it worked well. You never got the wrong gear as long as you pushed in the right direction. A snap movement told you that the lever was home and it was safe to release the clutch. Actually, clutchless

Dressy, ventilated wheel discs and narrow-stripe whitewall tires became available in 1957. Taillights are of second-generation design.

changes were easy, as long as you didn't get your revs too far wrong, say within a margin of 500.

Clutch action was positive. For smooth starts, a left foot with a sensitive feel for grip would be a big help. Oh yes, let's not forget reverse. It was quick, simple and foolproof. Press down on the knob, and keep pressing down while moving the lever out of neutral, left and back, into a slot next to second gear.

To sum up, it was a Volkswagen. There was just no getting away from that. Perhaps that point cannot be made too strongly, for its good points rather than the bad ones. Sure, the engine was noisy and underpowered. And it did not represent any peak of efficiency, for its fuel consumption was always at parity with cars in the next bigger category. But it had total reliability. It would start no matter what the climate, and once it ran, would keep running as long as there was fuel coming in.

There were VW service and parts all over the world. If the recommended preventive-maintenance schedule was a bit expensive, it was effective. And, at least Karmann-Ghia owners never had to worry about antifreeze, radiator leaks, hose clamps and water-pump seals.

Convertible, 1957 version, with the new wheels. The low build of the car becomes apparent by measuring against the model.

One of the assembly lines at the Karmann factory in Osnabrück. On the final assembly line, there was no separation between the Ghia models and the Beetle convertible.

Chapter Four

EVOLUTION OF THE KARMANN-BUILT VOLKSWAGENS

For many years the center for the Osnabrück-Wolfsburg collaboration was in Turin: Carrozzeria Ghia. It was part of the Ghia philosophy to provide a continuous flow of ideas for how to improve the product, even when there was little hope of having the ideas accepted. That philosophy intensified, if anything, after Mario Boano and Luigi Segre quarreled, and Boano left Ghia to set up his own coachbuilding shop in Turin in 1953. Naturally, Gian Paolo Boano went with his father.

Luigi Segre managed to find financial backing to take over Boano's holdings in Ghia, and the backers named three directors to the board: Dir. Rocca (managing director), Mrs. Marinetti and Dir. Moretti. Segre himself took the title of president, and personally handled the liaison with Karmann (Volkswagen was Karmann's client, and there was no direct contact between VW and Ghia).

Segre was an ambitious businessman, and formed a policy for strengthening Ghia's financial structure and income by expansion in the industrial sector. Moretti was head of the mechanical-engineering and instrument-making factory in Turin, close by the railroad yards immediately west of the central station. This company was known as O.S., and came to enjoy interlocking directorates with Ghia, so that when Moretti assumed his seat on the Ghia board, Luigi Segre was appointed to the O.S. board of directors.

At Segre's initiative, O.S. was transformed into O.S.I. (Officine Stampaggi Industriali, Industrial Pressings Factory), adding sheet-metal stampings to the existing product line of gears and gearboxes, and special auto parts. This was a first step in Segre's plan for providing Ghia with essential manufacturing capacity for series production of complete car

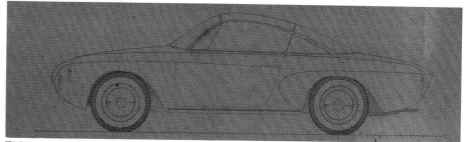

This proposal was for a restyled Karmann coupe, drawn by Sartorelli, probably in 1960. Outer skin was completely new, but chassis and basic body structure remained unchanged. Obvious cross-pollination with Exner (Chrysler) in the greenhouse area.

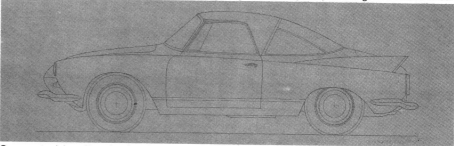

Suggested hardtop body, drawn by Tom Tjaarda in mid-1958. Karmann rejected it on the grounds that tailfins were not for Volkswagens (and no longer fashionable, anyway). Hardtop design with V-profile B-post was regarded as too American.

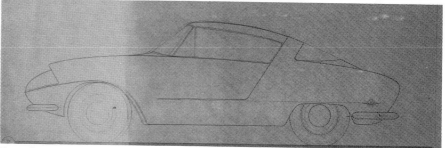

Pure fastback proposal for the Karmann coupe, drawn by Tom Tjaarda in 1958. His proportions were very sane, but the detail work and accent lines were redolent with Loewy influence. Considerable retooling would have been necessary.

bodies, and in 1956-57 Ghia moved into new premises in Via A. da Monte-feltro, adjacent to O.S.I.

But without the Boanos on the staff, Ghia was now short of styling capacity. Segre did not rush out to bring in new stylists. Instead he phoned a friend, Giovanni Savonuzzi, saying, "Will you please come here?" "And so," said Savonuzzi, "I became Ghia's director of body engineering."

Savonuzzi was an engineer with a diploma from the Polytechnical University of Turin, who had joined Fiat in 1938 as an experimental engineer in the aircraft engine test laboratory. After the war he linked up with Piero Dusio and was responsible for the production of the Cisitalia cars, in Italy up to 1952, and later in Argentina. He was working in the plastics industry back in Italy when Segre's call came.

It was natural for Savonuzzi to try to fill a vacuum wherever he saw it. With Segre's approval, he began to originate new designs. Several notable Ghia bodies from 1954-56 were Savonuzzi creations, including a futuristic-looking Jaguar, an Alfa Romeo and at least three Chrysler show cars, the Dart, the Gilda and the Norseman.

In 1956, Harry Chesebrough, then Chrysler's executive director of product planning and programming, invited Savonuzzi to come with him to Detroit and work for Chrysler, and he went. This time, Segre took a two-front approach, separating styling and engineering.

Ghia restyling proposal for the convertible, dated November 1958. Very clean lines, probably by Sartorelli. But the sharp angularity of the rear end did not marry with the rounded front.

Sergio Coggiola was named technical director for Karmann projects, which left him out of the pure design end, and primarily occupied with engineering drawings and prototype construction. For Karmann showed sufficient interest in certain Ghia ideas to order complete prototypes.

As early as 1954 Ghia had proposed a two-plus-two version of the coupe, with an extended roofline that gave the whole thing a curious sedan-like profile. Karmann had a prototype built by Ghia but when he showed it to the men of Wolfsburg, they wanted no part of it.

Before the end of 1954 Segre hired Sergio Sartorelli to work in Ghia's styling department. He was born at Alessandria in the Appennine foothills east of Asti in 1928 and, in addition to a considerable artistic talent, he held an engineering degree from the Turin Polytechnical University. Two years later, Sartorelli was named director of Ghia's styling department. He was soon to be joined by a young (twenty-four years of age) American, fresh out of the architect's school at the University of Michigan, by the name of Tom Tjaarda. His father, John Tjaarda, had been a major in-

Production-model 1959 convertible. Vent windows were never adopted for this model, nor for the Type 14 coupe.

fluence in Detroit styling trends in the thirties, but Tom wanted to learn the business in Italy, which turned out to be a blessing for Ghia.

The 1964 model convertible was almost impossible to distinguish from its 1959 forebear.

Rear view of the 1965 four-passenger convertible in a rustic German setting.

Upgraded Beetle convertible for 1965, with vented wheels and bigger engine.

Karmann-Ghia coupe and convertible, 1966 versions.

The Karmann Ghia convertible.

As a specialist in soft-top construction, Karmann had started work on a convertible version of the Ghia coupe as soon as there was engineering capacity available for the project. The "restyling" did not involve any of the exterior sheet metal below the belt line, and Ghia was not called in for this project. Considerable structural engineering work was undertaken, however, to reinforce the lower body in order to compensate for the loss of stiffness that the steel roof gave to the coupe. In spite of the deep and wide doors, this was accomplished in the body structure, as Karmann did not want to impose additional bending loads on the VW chassis frame.

The first version of the soft-top was made of a canvas-like fabric. It was tough, durable and relatively easy to clean, but bulky to fold. Plastic material was adopted about 1965, and the folded top pile shrank in size.

The 1966 convertible gone to the farmland.

Karmann production.

The arrival of the Karmann-Ghia models did not detract from the popularity of the Beetle convertible. On the contrary. In 1955, Karmann

The 1977-model four-passenger convertible was now available with radial-ply tires.

In 1956, Ghia proposed and Karmann built a removable-hardtop version of the coupe. Volkswagen vetoed it as a production model.

built 6,361 four-seater convertibles, which was a one-third increase over the previous year.

Production of the Karmann-Ghia coupe started slowly, and only thirty-seven were delivered to the dealers in August 1955. The public first saw the car at the Frankfurt auto show in September, and orders poured

Karmann built a spider in 1957, with lengthened rear deck, countersunk between the fenders. Again, no interest from Wolfsburg.

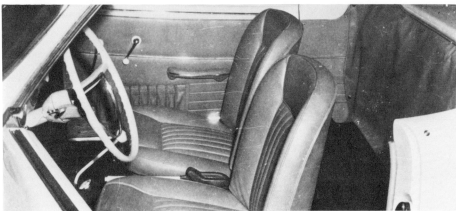

Prototype spider had the 1957-model steering wheel and bent-back gear lever, and no semblance of a rear seat. The spider prototype's top folded completely away below the metal cover. Doors, with slant-back window sill, had roll-down windows.

in. Karmann managed to speed up production quickly, and output reached 500 coupes in December 1955. For the first five months of production, Karmann built 1,280 Ghia coupes, but it took only fourteen months to pass the 10,000-car mark.

Production of the Karmann-Ghia convertible, Type 141 and 142, began on August 1, 1957. The official introduction was reserved for the international motor show in Frankfurt in September 1957. It was priced at 8,250 D-Marks, compared with 7,500 D-Marks for the coupe. Those prices were held for nearly four years, till August 1961, when they were reduced!

Climbing the Schwarzwald Hochstrasse, a curvy but fast road through the western Black Forest hills, with a 1959-model convertible.

Technical improvements by Volkswagen.

Right from the start, the Karmann-built Volkswagen models had automatically received the benefit of technical improvements made in the VW Beetle. To deal with these in chronological order, let me briefly recapitulate that hydraulic brakes were introduced on the 1950 models; synchromesh on second, third and fourth gears followed on the 1952 models;

Odd-style Ghia bumpers adorn 1958 facelift proposal (left). On the right, the 1955 production model.

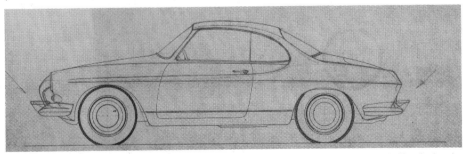

Ghia restyling study for the Karmann coupe, probably from early 1958. Basic body structure would not be affected. Key elements in the new skin included big simulated split grille, C-post and rear window profile, freshened-up rear fenders, all-new bumpers.

New body for the coupe was drawn by Sartorelli of Ghia in 1961, but was doomed to remain in the prototype stage.

tire size went from 5.00-16 in 1951 to 5.60-15 for 1952; engine displacement was increased from 1131 to 1192 cc for 1954; low-profile fuel tank was adopted for 1956; and tubeless tires were standardized for 1957.

For 1958, a flat accelerator pedal, hinged at the bottom, replaced the former suspended roller-rod. At the same time, the front brake shoes and drums were widened from 30 to 40 mm, giving increased friction area, about 620 cm² or 96 square inches. For the 1958 Karmann-Ghia models, the front fenders were raised and the headlamps moved upward. New, wider air scoops (air intakes) enhanced the nose.

Technical progress also flowed from the Karmann-Ghia back to the pure Wolfsburg products. For instance, the front stabilizer bar from the sports-model chassis was adopted for the Beetle and four-seater convertible in August 1959 (1960 models).

New items for all the 1960 models included a redesigned steering wheel, with a dished-for-safety profile. In March 1960, a hydraulic damper was fitted on the steering linkage, to prevent road shocks from causing wheel fight. For European markets, the 1960 export models (including the Karmann-Ghias) could be ordered with the Saxomat vacuum-operated automatic clutch as an extra-cost option.

Rear view of the Sartorelli design, with its strong horizontal emphasis that made the car look lower and wider.

Prototype for the 1959-model coupe, with vent panes in the front doors. Built by Karmann in 1957-58. Rear view shows the odd taillights that Volkswagen rejected out of hand.

Big changes were made in the VW 1200 (1192 cc) engine for 1961, to the extent that it was almost a new engine. The cylinder spacing was increased by 10 mm (0.4 inch) to provide more cooling capacity, and the crankshaft was redesigned with bigger main and crankpin bearings. The combustion chamber was revised, with valves inclined at nine degrees to the cylinder axis (instead of parallel), and valve sizes were increased: Intake

The profile that might have been. Volkswagen turned it down, but Ghia used some of the same lines on bodies built for Fiat, notably the 2300-S.

A well-balanced article, the Ghia prototype designed by Sartorelli in 1961.

valve head diameter went from 30 mm to 31.5 mm (1.18 to 1.24 inches), while the same measurement for the exhaust valves went from 28 mm to 30 mm (1.10 to 1.18 inches).

A modified camshaft featured higher lift, and new tappets were mushroom-shaped instead of barrel-shaped. The tappets were rotated by the cams through off-center actuation.

Bore and stroke remained unchanged, but the compression ratio was raised to 7.0:1, giving a 4 hp increase in output:

1961-model 1200 engine

Maximum output	34 hp DIN @ 3600 rpm
	40 hp SAE gross @ 3900 rpm
Maximum torque	8.4 m-kg @ 2000 rpm
	58 lb. ft. SAE gross @ 2400 rpm

A different carburetor, Solex 28 PICT, with automatic choke and acceleration pump, was adopted.

To go with the new engine, all Type 1 VW's also received an improved four-speed transmission, with synchromesh also on first gear, and helical-cut teeth on all gears.

1965-model production coupe with two-tone color scheme.

The final drive ratio, for all export models and Karmann-Ghia cars, was changed from 4.43 to 4.375:1, which represented a 1.24 percent slow-down of the engine speed in relation to the road speed. To make sure that the cars had adequate tractive effort to start on a thirty-percent gradient with a full load, the first-gear ratio was changed from 3.60 to 3.80:1, and to guard against a loss of top-gear performance, the fourth-gear (overdrive) ratio was altered from 0.82 to 0.89:1. Top speed for the Beetle went up from 110 to 116 km/h (68 to 72 mph), and the Karmann-Ghia coupe was capable of an easy 125 km/h (77.5 mph).

The fuel tank gauge first appeared on the 1962 models. Until then, all you had was a dipstick (and a reserve tap).

Additional horsepower.

A larger engine became optional for the Beetle (Type 113) for 1966, and was adopted as standard in the Karmann-Ghia models. Outwardly it was indistinguishable from the 1192 cc unit, but its displacement was

The 1966-model Karmann-Ghia coupe.

Fuel gauge was included, left of the speedometer, on the 1966 models.

Pockets were added as the Ghia's door equipment and upholstery became more luxurious.

1285 cc, due to a longer stroke. The enlargement was obtained, quite simply, by fitting the crankshaft from the Type 3 engine (see Chapter Five) with its 69 mm stroke (the 1200 had a stroke of 64 mm) in the Type 1 crankcase.

The carburetor was correspondingly enlarged, the new one being a Solex 30 PICT, and the compression ratio was again increased, now to 7.3:1. Intake valve head diameter was increased from 31.5 to 33.0 mm (1.24 to 1.30 inches).

VW 1300 engine

Maximum output	40 hp DIN @ 4000 rpm
	50 hp SAE gross @ 4600 rpm
Maximum torque	8.9 m-kg DIN @ 2000 rpm
	69 lb.ft. SAE gross @ 2600 rpm

The more Volkswagen increased the power and performance of the Type 1, the more its weaknesses became apparent. The rear swing axle, coupled with the mass concentration of the rear-mounted engine, posed a serious handling and stability problem.

At first, Volkswagen attacked it only by half-measures. The first significant improvement came with the 1966 models, when the rear track was widened by 58 mm (2.28 inches) to 1,339 mm (52.7 inches), and a compensating spring was added to the rear suspension. This was a transverse

A look into the 1966 convertible cockpit.

torsion bar, intended to permit normal deflections in jounce, while preventing excessive rebound. In rebound deflections, the swing axles went into a hopeless positive-camber position, and the spring was a moderately effective cure.

The 1966 Karmann-Ghia models underwent a number of minor changes. An alternator replaced the former AC generator, so as to provide battery charging even at idle speed. The air cleaner was moved, so as to necessitate a lateral displacement of the battery. The light and wiper/washer switches were moved to the left side of the speedometer, and the dashboard ashtrays were brought into conformity with the Type 3 design.

For 1967, the Karmann-Ghia models and the up-market Beetles (including the Type 15 four-passenger convertible) were given yet a bigger engine. This time it was the complete cylinders from the Type 3 (83 x 69 mm) that were fitted on the crankcase of the Type 1 engine, raising the displacement to 1493 cc. That raised the engine weight (as installed) to 114 kg (251 pounds).

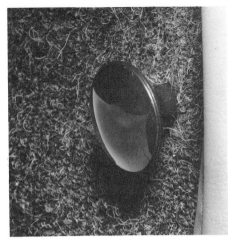

Pull-button release for the engine cover.

Complete interior luggage compartment and rear seatback of the coupe were carpeted.

Heater controls for 1966 remained on the central tunnel, next to the handbrake.

With a padded dash, the passenger's grab rail was made of softer material.

VW Type 14 1500 engine

Maximum output	44 hp DIN @ 4000 rpm
	53 hp SAE gross @ 4200 rpm
Maximum torque	10.2 m-kg DIN @ 2000 rpm
	78 lb. ft. SAE gross @ 2600 rpm
Camshaft:	
Base circle	31 mm
Lift, intake	7.78 mm
Lift, exhaust	7.37 mm
Inlet opens	7°30' BTC
Inlet closes	37° ABC
Exhaust opens	44°30' BBC
Exhaust closes	4° ATC

To go with this engine, the final drive ratio was changed to 4.125:1. The gearbox ratios remained unchanged except for a "longer" third gear, which went from 1.32:1 to 1.26:1.

The Karmann-Ghia models were capable of reaching 132 km/h (82 mph) and the four-seater convertible, 127 km/h (79 mph).

No suspension and steering changes this year; but for the first time on Type 1 Volkswagens, front disc brakes became optional. Cars for North American markets were equipped with a dual hydraulic circuit, as required by law. The optional disc brake system had solid rotors with an external diameter of 277 mm (10.9 inches) and brake pads having a friction area of 72 cm^2 (11.2 sq. in.). There was no power assist, but the pedal arm ratio had been lowered to 210/33 mm on all models to ease the pedal effort.

For 1968, all VW engines going to the U.S. were equipped with a dashpot on the carburetor linkage to retard the throttle closing when the driver suddenly took his foot off the accelerator, and an auxiliary air-injection reactor system on the exhaust manifold, with a belt-driven air pump.

There were no basic engine modifications, but a semiautomatic transmission became optional. It consisted of a hydraulic torque converter in place of the friction clutch, coupled with a manually shifted three-speed gearbox. It used the three upper ratios of the standard VW four-speed transmission (2.06 first, 1.26 second, 0.89:1 top) with a final drive ratio of 4.375:1.

For 1969, both convertibles and the two-seater coupe were built only with the 1500 engine. All models went from a 6-volt to a 12-volt electrical system. All cars (except the 1200 series) equipped with semiautomatic transmission featured a dramatically new rear suspension system.

Here, the swing axles had been discarded in favor of a modern design with semitrailing arms and double-jointed half-shafts (as pioneered by BMW). But instead of BMW's coil springs, Volkswagen had chosen transverse torsion bars, true to form.

The torsion bars gave a wheel rate of 21 kg/cm (117.6 pounds per inch) on the Karmann-Ghia models and 24.4 kg/cm (136.6 pounds per inch) on the four-seater convertible. They were supplemented by double-acting telescopic shock absorbers, and the compensating spring had been eliminated, for the roll stiffness was high enough without it (33.8 m-kg or 244 lb. ft. per degree on the Karmann-Ghia and 39.3 m-kg or 283 lb.ft. per degree on the four-seater convertible).

This was the biggest and most effective suspension change ever undertaken by Volkswagen. David Phipps tested it, and immediately said that "now the VW handles better than a Porsche." With all due respect to Porsche, he had a point, in that the VW's road behavior had suddenly become irreproachable. The complete change of rear suspension geometry was enough to accomplish this near-miracle, with no change in weight distribution or tire size. It's a great pity that it was adopted only for a small percentage of Volkswagen's production.

Ghia's modernization proposals.

Throughout the sixties, Ghia had not stopped sending to Karmann new suggestions for modernizing the VW sports coupe. These suggestions ranged from simple facelift styling sketches to actual prototype cars. Before the start of the seventies, it might have been thought wise to replace the original Karmann-Ghia body with an updated design from the same source, and one could easily have concluded, then, that it would help perpetuate the production life of the car. In hindsight, that would not have been proved correct, for the advance of car design and automotive engineering was quickly catching up with the Beetle, and VW was headed for sweeping and fundamental changes in its product line and manufacturing program.

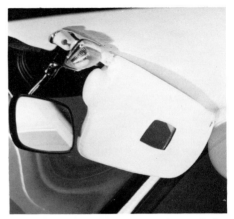

Vanity mirror in the sun visor of the coupe; dome light above rearview mirror.

There was no way anyone at Ghia could know that. Even Karmann, who was to participate in Volkswagen's plans by building the Scirocco as well as the Golf convertible, was kept in the dark about the extent and scope of the coming revolution.

Karmann in fact commissioned Ghia to build a complete, running prototype of a design done by Filippo Sapino in 1963-64. Between the time of the original Karmann-Ghia and the mid-sixties, a tragic event had caused a major upheaval in the Ghia organization. The tragedy came in the form of Luigi Segre's being felled by disease in February 1963.

At his death, the other board members appealed to Gino Rovere, former chairman of the Maserati company (prior to its being absorbed by Orsi), to take over. He did, but died about a year later.

In the space of that year, Sartorelli and Tjaarda had left Ghia. Sartorelli went to O.S.I., where he worked for three years, and finally joined Fiat's styling center in 1968. Tom Tjaarda found a job with Pininfarina, but returned to Ghia in 1968 as styling director.

Sergio Coggiola stayed with Ghia, continuing as body-engineering chief for Karmann projects. Filippo Sapino was one of Ghia's glowing new styling talents, hired in 1960, when he was only twenty years old. He was both original and prolific, and started Ghia's styling trends off in new directions. In his 1963-64 Karmann-Ghia proposal, the styling left no hint

Ghia proposal for fully rebodied Karmann coupe, drawn by Filippo Sapino in 1963-64. Styling left no hint of rear-mounted engine, but a dimensional check proves that there was space for all vital chassis and power train components.

of rear-mounted engine, but a dimensional check proved that there was space for all vital chassis and power train components. Sapino continued to make valuable contributions to Ghia styling until he went to Pininfarina in 1967.

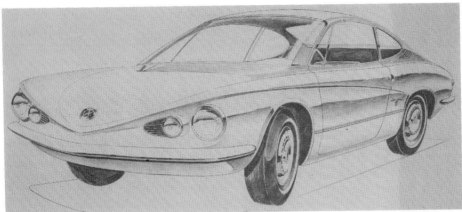

Three-dimensional view as first visualized by Sapino. Front end was aerodynamically advantageous, but just about eliminated luggage space. Karmann may have found untold manufacturing problems in this concept.

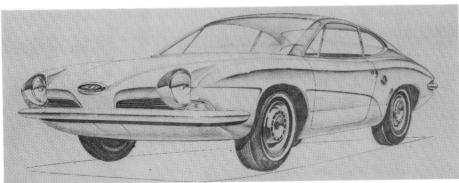

Later alternative version of Sapino's proposal. Main differences were in ovalized VW emblem, grilles pulled down to bumper level, recessed headlamps, elimination of C-post base air intakes.

Running the Ghia company was a task that fell to Giacomo Gaspardo Moro when Segre died. He was not a car man at all, but had worked fifteen years in Rome as a film and television producer. Segre knew him, having had contracts over publicity matters for many years, such as featuring Ghia-bodied cars on the screen. "One day," Giacomo Gaspardo Moro told me, "the phone rang in my office, and it was Segre. He asked me, in that special way he had, 'come with me tomorrow,' so in April 1960, I joined Ghia as assistant to the president."

Moro served as general manager of Carrozzeria Ghia from 1963 to 1967, and in 1965 expanded the styling staff by hiring a young man named Giorgetto Giugiaro away from Bertone. He was not involved with the Volks-wagen projects, however, but spent his time mainly drawing bodies for new Maserati cars.

In the spring of 1967, an American firm, Rowan Controllers, Inc., acquired full ownership of Carrozzeria Ghia and installed Alejandro De Tomaso as president. De Tomaso was a controversial figure in Italy, a rac-ing driver from Argentina, racing car constructor in Modena, with in-

The last Ghia proposal ever made to Karmann on a VW chassis was the Type 1 con-vertible of 1967, designed by Giugiaro.

dustrial ambitions, married to the sister of the president of Rowan Controllers, Inc.

Giacomo Gaspardo Moro resigned. Sapino and Giugiaro went to work elsewhere. Sergio Coggiola decided it was time to start his own establishment, and opened a shop in Nichelino.

The cooperation between Karmann and Ghia drifted out of existence. Tom Tjaarda went back to Ghia, where he designed the Ford-powered Pantera. In 1971, Ford bought control of Ghia. In the meantime, Filippo Sapino, after two years with Pininfarina, had joined Ford as head of a separate styling center at Bruino, and in 1973 returned to Via A. da Montefeltro as general manager of Ghia Operations, a division of Ford Motor Company.

The twilight of the Karmann-Ghia.

An additional version of the Type 1 engine became optional for the 1970 models. Its displacement of 1584 cc (96.6 cubic inches) was obtained by boring out the cylinders to 85.5 mm (3.37 inches), and keeping the 1500 crankshaft. The compression ratio was 7.5:1.

Flat, four-spoke "safety" steering wheel came into use in 1970 (for the 1971 models).

A nostalgic look back from the last convertible to its ancestor of 1938.

92

VW 1600 engine

Power output	47 hp DIN @ 4000 rpm
	57 hp SAE gross @ 4400 rpm
Maximum torque	10.6 m-kg DIN @ 2200 rpm
	81.5 lb.ft. SAE gross @ 3000 rpm

Valve timing and valve sizes were the same as in the 1500 engine, and the same Solex 30 PICT carburetor was fitted.

Both the 1500 and 1600 engines were offered in the four-passenger convertible as well as the Karmann-Ghia models, with a choice of four-speed manual and three-speed semiautomatic transmission. In all cases, a final drive ratio of 4.125:1 was used.

Top speed with the 1600 engine and four-speed gearbox increased to 130 km/h (81.5 mph) for the four-passenger Cabriolet and 135 km/h (84 mph) for the Karmann-Ghia models. Combined with the semiautomatic transmission, it was slower (a 7.5 percent drop in top speed) and fuel consumption went up by about five percent, on average.

Acceleration times shrank to thirteen seconds for the 0-80 km/h (50 mph) run, and twenty-one seconds for reaching 100 km/h (62 mph) from standstill, with the four-speed version. With the semiautomatic transmission, the car took fifteen seconds to reach 80 km/h and twenty-three seconds to get to 100 km/h.

Starting late in 1970, Karmann-Ghia models for the U.S. market were built with the 1600 engine exclusively. At the same time, the 1600 replaced the 1500 in all other models. Its output was raised to 50 hp DIN (60 hp SAE gross) for the 1971 model year.

Big changes took place in the Beetle chassis that year, with the introduction of the 1302 S, having a new front suspension system and a 20 mm (four inches) longer wheelbase. It was marketed in the U.S. under the name Super-Beetle.

The new front suspension system was of the MacPherson type, with a single lower control arm per wheel, inclined spring legs housing telescopic shock absorbers and carrying concentric coil springs. Front track increased to 1,379 mm (54.3 inches), and the fuel tank was redesigned, with its capacity increased to 45 liters (11.6 gallons). A new steering gear with a 17.8:1 ratio was adopted, giving 2.65 turns, lock-to-lock, with greatly improved steering angles: thirty-five degrees on the outside wheel and forty degrees on the inside wheel, shortening the turning diameter to 9.6 m (31.5 feet).

While the Type 1302 chassis was immediately adopted for the four-passenger convertible, the Karmann-Ghia body shape and structure could not accept the MacPherson front end, and continued with the old trailing arm and torsion bar system, on the usual 2,400 mm wheelbase.

Engine modifications for 1972 included wider oil channels (for better cooling) and tighter control over the oil pressure; adoption of oil-bath air cleaners and a new preheating device taking account of both temperature and load. The engine mounting system was improved, in the interest of reducing the noise level inside the car.

The Karmann-Ghia sustained some sheet-metal changes at the front end, to accommodate the new 2.5 mph bumper demanded by the U.S. safety standards, and all models were fitted with padded steering wheels.

Rear view of the last Type 14 convertible, showing the 2.5 mph bumpers and new taillights.

The front disc brake system from the Type 3 was standardized for all models powered by the 1600 engine, and made optional for the 1300. This system had considerably bigger discs, with an outside diameter of 278 mm (10.9 inches) and a friction pad area of 80 cm² (12.4 square inches). On the Karmann-Ghia models fitted with the 1600 engine and four-speed gearbox, the final drive ratio was changed to 3.875:1, which raised the top speed to 145 km/h (90 mph). Ironically, this model continued with the swing axles, while the semiautomatic version was equipped with the semitrailing arm system.

In August 1972, Type 1303 replaced the Type 1302, and this affected the four-passenger convertible body. It was given a larger and more curved windshield, new front seats with better lateral support and new mounting

In 1971 the four-passenger convertible went to VW 1303 chassis specifications, with MacPherson front suspension.

rails. The gear lever and handbrake were moved to fit better with the new seating.

All models powered by the 1600 engine were equipped with front disc brakes.

Gearing changes included a lower first gear for all four-speed transmissions (3.78:1) for surer uphill starts with a full load, and for all models except the Karmann-Ghia, a new top gear ratio of 0.93:1, which improved the top gear performance. The Karmann-Ghia models continued with the 0.88:1 top gear, so as to avoid any loss in top speed. On the semiautomatic option, a parking pawl was added.

The Karmann-Ghia models were also fitted with wider tires. The new size was 6.00-15, tubeless, four-ply rating.

Close-up view of the front suspension on the 1971-model 1303 and convertible.

1972-model 1303 convertible with the top closed—a high quality construction throughout.

96

New emission-control equipment caused a drop in the output of the 1600 engine for cars sold in the U.S. market. At the same time, the industry switched from SAE gross to SAE net horsepower:

1973 1600 U.S. version

Maximum output	38 hp DIN @ 4000 rpm
	46 hp SAE net @ 4000 rpm
Maximum torque	10.2 m-kg DIN @ 2000 rpm
	71 lb.ft. SAE net @ 2000 rpm

On the 1974-model Karmann-Ghia, top gear was brought in line with the rest of the VW cars (0.93:1). Cars equipped with front disc brakes had a revised design, with floating calipers (for lower manufacturing cost).

Engine modifications were minor: a new cylinder head alloy, revised exhaust muffler and improved preheating of the air for the carburetor. The 1300 engine was no longer available in the Karmann-Ghia, even for European markets. All of them came with the 1600 in their last year of production.

The other Karmann-Ghia: the Brazilian coupe, introduced in 1970.

Production of the Karmann-Ghia was discontinued in July 1974. Why? First, because Type 1 was being phased out, and the chassis would not be available for very long into the future. Second, because its replacement, the Scirocco, was ready.

The total production of Karmann-Ghia models amounted to 387,975 cars, including 23,577 Brazilian-made coupes (for in 1960 Karmann had set up a branch factory at Sao Bernardo do Campo, conveniently close to the huge Volkswagen do Brasil plant—under the title Karmann-Ghia do Brasil S.A.).

In its German factories, Karmann produced 364,398 Ghia-designed VW Type 1 sports models: 283,501 coupes and 80,897 convertibles.

Deliveries to North America began in 1956. Its East Coast port-of-entry price was only $2,395, and on the West Coast, $2,475. Because of production bottlenecks, only 2,452 Karmann-Ghia coupes were sold in the U.S. in 1956.

The Brazilian coupe was a true fastback; only the louvers above the taillights betrayed the rear engine position.

How the taillights grew! First and last Karmann-Ghia coupes, seen side by side.

During 1961, Volkswagen dealers in the U.S. sold nearly 9,500 Karmann-Ghias, including over 1,000 convertibles. Sales then stabilized around 10,000 units a year, after the price had been cut to $2,295 in 1962. The all-time record was set in 1970, with sales of some 38,000 Karmann-Ghias. In 1973-74 the demand dwindled and stockpiling ensued. Karmann completed only 1,500 VW-Ghias in 1974, but almost 8,000 were sold in the U.S. that year.

The four-passenger Type 15 convertible was kept in production until January 10, 1979. The last one was number 331,847. The "topless beetle" had had a thirty-year career, which would have become increasingly difficult to prolong. VW Type 15 convertible production had fallen to 18,511 in 1978. Of these, more than half (9,857) was sold in the U.S. while nearly one third (6,027) was absorbed in the German market. It is noteworthy that 1,326 were sold in Italy, where Beetle sales were notoriously low.

The principal considerations behind the final demise of the Beetle convertible are easily explained: The car no longer met the U.S. emission-

The last-built convertible remains in Karmann's collection. Stylized parking and turn signal lights were first adopted on the 1971 models.

control and traffic safety regulations, and it would have been very costly to undertake modifications for that purpose.

Withdrawing from the U.S. but continuing to build the Beetle convertible for European markets would have meant throttling production to one third of former levels, leaving the plant underused and raising the unit cost. A higher price would have further restricted the demand for this type of car.

The possibility of producing the Beetle convertible in Mexico was rejected because the Puebla plant built only the 1200 model, and the convertible was based on the Type 1303.

Gerd Gieseke (left) and Gottfried Niemann pose with the first and last Karmann-Ghia coupes.

Some marketing studies were made while the Golf convertible was still under development, regarding the possibility of selling it side by side with the Beetle convertible. They were not conclusive, however, and the decision was facilitated by the instant market success of the Golf convertible. That effectively sealed the fate of the Type 15 four-passenger convertible.

The final models from 1974, side by side.

Chapter Five

NORDHOFF'S UP-MARKET VOLKSWAGEN

Rumors about a modernized Volkswagen, or a Beetle successor, had been circulating for years, and were gaining strength year by year since 1955. The need for a new product seemed obvious to most industry observers. Some found it incredible that Heinz Nordhoff could continue to rely on a prewar design to provide the bulk of Volkswagen's revenues for an indefinite future.

It would have been incredible, but it was not the case, for the shrewd Nordhoff had prepared contingency plans well in advance. Porsche engineers had in fact been working on a new Volkswagen project since 1953-54, and the broad lines of its layout, design and technical makeup were pretty well defined by 1957.

Marketing studies made throughout the fifties reflected Germany's economic miracle, as consumers at all levels of society prospered under the liberal free-enterprise policies of economics minister Ludwig Erhard. Car buyers were moving up-market very quickly, deserting the "bubble cars" and other mini-cars in favor of solidly middle-class machinery.

The market forced Goggomobil, NSU, Goliath and Lloyd to make bigger and more powerful models, with higher-grade interiors and a long list of luxury and convenience options. Those who did not follow (Gutbrod, Messerschmitt, Fuldamobil, Kleinschnittger, Champion) dropped out of the car business.

Projections of economic trends convinced Nordhoff that the next Volkswagen must inevitably be a better-equipped, roomier, more powerful and higher-priced car, if it were to reach a sales volume sufficient to occupy a major share of Wolfsburg's production capacity (as the Beetle did).

The project was repeatedly delayed, however, because every time Nordhoff weighed the question of when to start tooling up for the new car, he looked at the Beetle sales statistics, whose strength was most reassuring, and the urgency of getting the proposed Beetle replacement into production never became evident to him.

Yet he knew that its time had to come, and Type 3 (the Transporter/Microbus van was Type 2) finally got the green light. But by 1959-60, Nordhoff was hedging his bet: Type 3 was not to replace the Beetle immediately, but be built side by side with it, as long as the free market forces indicated a continued need for both types.

This is, incidentally, another bit of evidence to prove the invalidity of the uninformed accusations of Nordhoff for his "monoculture." He was, in fact, expanding the range on a scale that compared with Ford's addition of the Falcon to its manufacturing program.

Some of Nordhoff's basic requirements for Type 3 played a part in shaping it. His demand for more room (with no change in wheelbase) could best be met by going to a box-shaped rather than egg-shaped body shell.

Low-profile engine for the 1500 was obtained by moving the fan down to the crankshaft, and lowering the electrical accessories.

103

The profile ended up not unlike the Ford Anglia/Prefect introduced in 1954.

Because Nordhoff insisted on building a station wagon based on the sedan body, something that was unthinkable with the Beetle body structure and its high engine profile, a new low-profile engine had to be developed.

Horsepower requirement, with due observation of the Volkswagen understress policy, was calculated to need about 1500 cc. The 1200 cc Beetle engine was then at the limit allowed by its cylinder spacing, chosen for 985 cc, with a margin for about twenty-percent enlargement. In the new engine for Type 3, the cylinder spacing was chosen so that enlargement up to 1700 cc was possible, with the same crankshaft.

The biggest visible change in the engine was the revised package size. To lower the engine profile, the mountings that carried the cooling fan and generator above the cylinders had to be separated from the main engine castings. Instead, a smaller-diameter fan (with greater airflow capacity) was placed at the rear end of the crankshaft, and the generator was belt-driven from the pulley at the flywheel end of the crankshaft (front).

VW Type 3 engine and transmission in side view. It weighed 123 kg (2 lbs.) in twin-carb version.

With the new engine layout, it became possible to get a normal trunk, with its floor low enough to carry a big suitcase—and still close the lid. For the Variant station wagon, the tailgate opened to a load platform only about eight inches above bumper height. But the new engine was considerably heavier: 122 kg (269 pounds).

For Type 3, Nordhoff also took the initiative toward developing a four-passenger convertible in collaboration with Karmann, and to have Ghia propose styling for both a sports coupe and sports convertible. At that, any remnants of a theory of a one-model policy on Nordhoff's part must surely explode.

Beetle heritage was evident in the Type 3 chassis, of course, but there was no interchangeability of parts. It was just part of the Porsche/VW philosophy at the time that it would not be a Volkswagen unless it had an air-cooled rear-mounted engine, a "backbone" frame and torsion-bar suspension with trailing links in front and swing axles at the back. Porsche remained faithful to the same principles for its own production models up to 1964.

Once it became clear that the 1500 (Type 3) would not be a Beetle successor but a companion model to the Beetle, manufacturing considerations began to play a more significant role, all arguing in favor of retaining the greatest possible similarity between the two cars, so as to allow sharing

Karmann four-seater convertible on standard VW 1500 model, 1961. Its silhouette closely followed the all-steel sedan body profile.

of machining lines, assembly sequences and methods and the materials flow in general. In fact, it became vital for cost control.

The first pictures of the new model leaked to the motoring press in March 1961, and a group of American journalists was invited to Wolfsburg in June 1961 to see and drive it. They saw only the two-door sedan and the Variant, however. Those models went into full production on September 1, 1961.

The fact that the car had a rear-mounted engine was well concealed, for the louvers at the C-post base could be taken for ventilation air extractors.

Open-top appearance of the 1500. The folded top almost disappeared below the belt line, and front door vent panes were standard.

Type 3 four-seater convertible.

Built by Karmann, the four-seater convertible was introduced at the Frankfurt auto show in mid-September 1961. But the reception was so cool that it never became a true production model.

It was a Karmann conversion of the basic sedan, using all the standard sheet metal below the belt line. The top looked neat when it was up (slightly British, some critics said), and folded away to almost nothing behind the rear seat.

SPECIFICATIONS
Volkswagen four-passenger convertible   Type 3
Valid as of June 11, 1961
Architecture
Rear-mounted engine, rear-wheel drive. Fuel tank and spare wheel between front wheels. Luggage space between front wheels and above engine.
Dimensions

Wheelbase	2400 mm	94.5 in.
Track, front	1310 mm	51.2 in.
Track, rear	1346 mm	53.0 in.
Overall length	4225 mm	166.3 in.
Overall width	1605 mm	63.2 in.
Overall height (unladen)	1475 mm	58.1 in.
Ground clearance	149 mm	5.9 in.
Minimum turn diameter	11.4 m	37.4 ft.
Weight		
Dry weight	880 kg	1940 lb.
Payload capacity	370 kg	816 lb.

Controls remained typical of Volkswagen, but there was a new look to the instrument panel.

Maximum all-up weight	1250 kg	2756 lb.
Maximum front end load	495 kg	1091 lb.
Maximum rear end load	755 kg	1665 lb.

Engine

Layout	Horizontally opposed four-cylinder with individual finned cylinders screwed into a common crankcase.
Cooling	Forced air: shrouded fan on a vertical shaft above the cylinders driven by helical gears.
Bore	83mm 3.27 in.
Stroke	69 mm 2.72 in.
Displacement	1493 cc 91.1 cu.in.
Compression ratio	7.5:1
Carburetor	1 Solex horizontal 32 PHN-1
Valves	Overhead, inclined at 9° from the cylinder axis, operated by pushrods and rocker arms.
Valve timing	Inlet opens 7°30' BTC
	Inlet closes 37° ABC
	Exhaust opens 44°30' BBC
	Exhaust closes 4° ATC
Camshaft	Located directly below the crankshaft and driven by spur gears. Cast iron with integral cams.
Crankshaft	One-plane forged steel, counterweighted, running in 4 main bearings.
Connecting rods	Forged steel, I-beam profile.
Pistons	Cast aluminum with steel insert.
Output	45 hp DIN @ 3800 rpm, 54 hp SAE gross @ 4200 rpm
Torque	10.8 m-kg @ 2000 rpm, 83 lb.ft. SAE gross @ 2800 rpm

Drive train

Clutch	Single dry plate
Transmission	4-speed manual gearbox, synchromesh on all forward speeds.

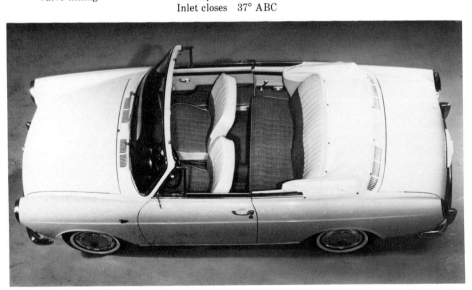

Rear seat room was unhampered by the folded top. Luggage space above the engine also remained intact.

Gear ratios	1st, 3.80:1; 2nd, 2.06; 3rd, 1.32; 4th, 0.89; Rev, 3.88.
Final drive	Spiral bevel
Final drive ratio	4.125:1

Chassis

Front suspension	Dual trailing links (upper and lower) per wheel, with transverse torsion bars, stabilizer bar and telescopic shock absorbers.
Rear suspension	Pendulum-type swing axles with trailing arms, transverse torsion bars, transverse camber-compensating bar and telescopic shock absorbers.

Steering	Worm-and-roller, with hydraulic damper on the steering linkage.
Steering gear ratio	18.5:1
Overall steering ratio	14.9:1
Turns, lock-to-lock	2.8
Maximum steering angle	27° (outside wheel), 30° (inside wheel)
Steering wheel diameter	400 mm 15.75 in.
Brakes	Four-wheel hydraulic w/o power assist, dual hydraulic circuits, split between front and rear. Drums front and rear, duo-servo shoes in front drums.

Fog lamps below the bumper were nonstandard. Roadster in the background is 1938 Ford Eifel with Karmann body. Further left, prewar Adler convertibles by Karmann.

Drum diameter	248 mm	9.8 in.
Lining area	960 cm²	
Wheels and tires	Tire size	6.00-15
	Rim size	4½J-15
Dynamic roll radius	309 mm	12.2 in.
Inflation pressure	1.2 Bar (front)	18 psi, 1.8 Bar (rear) 26 psi

Performance

Top speed	130 km/h	81.5 mph

Acceleration	0-50 km/h (31 mph) 5.0 sec.
	0-60 km/h (37 mph) 7.8 sec.
	0-80 km/h (50 mph) 15.5 sec.
	0-100 km/h (62 mph) 24.5 sec.
Fuel consumption	(DIN 70030 calculated average) 8.3 liters per 100 km (28.3 mpg)
Hill-climbing ability	1st gear, 45% gradient; 2nd, 24%; 3rd, 14%; 4th, 8%.

In August 1963, Volkswagen introduced the 1500 S with a high-compression (8.5:1), twin-carburetor version of the same engine (Solex 32 PDSIT), which improved both performance and fuel economy.

VW Type 31 1500-S

Maximum output	54 hp DIN @ 4200 rpm
	66 hp SAE gross @ 4800 rpm
Maximum torque	10.8 m-kg DIN @ 2400 rpm
	83 lb.ft. SAE Gross @ 3000 rpm

A fastback VW 1600 coupe was proposed in 1965. Karmann built the prototype to Ghia designs.

A further Type 3 variation, the VW 1600 TL coupe, followed in August 1965 as a 1966 model. It was a fastback version of the basic two-door sedan, with a bored-out engine that replaced the 1500 in all Type 3 models for 1966.

VW Type 31 1600

Bore	85.5 mm	3.37 in.
Stroke	69 mm	2.72 in.
Displacement	1584 cc	96.7 cu.in.
Compression ratio	7.7:1	
Carburetor	Two downdraft Solex 32 PDSIT	
Maximum output	54 hp DIN @ 4000 rpm, 65 hp SAE gross @ 4600 rpm	
Maximum torque	11.2 m-kg DIN @ 2200 rpm, 87 lb.ft. SAE gross @ 2800 rpm	
Top speed	135 km/h	84 mph

All 1966-model Type 3 cars were built with front disc brakes, having a rotor diameter of 277 mm (10.9 inches).

Front view of the fastback prototype shows proportions that later became fashionable in America.

Type 3 Karmann-Ghia models.

By mid-1960, the final version of the new 1500 coupe began to emerge from preliminary sketches. In profile, the car was beautifully balanced, except for perhaps a lack of concordance between the windshield and rear

One of the first 1500 coupes built is now in Karmann's collection.

Headlamp and fender treatment and the tall windshield curving into the roof were items seen on production-model Plymouth and Dodge cars of the same era.

Rear view of the Karmann-Ghia 1500 coupe shows the flat deck and enlarged glass area.

Nose of the 1500 Karmann-Ghia coupe was a Sartorelli creation. Some family resemblance to the Type 14 was preserved.

window angles. The greenhouse looked modern with its extended glass area, but the straight accent lines along the fenders fought with the roughness of the front.

The curlicues on the nose were never well received by the public (Americans had not liked them when something similar had appeared on Plymouth and Dodge grilles).

The prime designer of this car was Sergio Sartorelli. Among his assistants at the time was a young artist named Bruno Sacco, who became styling chief for Mercedes-Benz in 1972. Sergio Coggiola was in charge of prototype construction, working in close liaison with the Karmann engineers.

Coggiola made an interesting remark that sheds some light on Luigi Segre's ambitions: "I think Segre had the intention of producing complete

Preliminary study for the VW 1500 (Type 3) Karmann-Ghia coupe, drawn by Sartorelli in mid-1960. Curlicues around headlamps were pulled toward the center; dual headlamps gave way to singles; the lip above the rear window was removed; and the rear fender lines were softened for the production model.

bodies for a VW 1500 sports model in Torino." Apparently there were preparations for some VW-related production going on at O.S.I. at the time, and Coggiola's remark could well explain that.

Eventually, the Type 34 coupe was built only in the Karmann works. The convertible never went into production at all. Production of the coupe did not begin at introduction time, but had to wait until March 1962.

At Osnabrück, Johannes Beeskow was chief body engineer on the Type 34 coupe. He had formerly worked for Friedrich Rometsch in Berlin, and had done the Rometsch car in 1951 on VW chassis.

Ghia proposed a clip-on roof for a convertible hardtop based on VW's Type 3. Drawing by Sartorelli, 1962-63. Curlicues are gone, replaced by wide horizontal grille units on either side of pointed nose.

SPECIFICATIONS
Volkswagen two-passenger Karmann-Ghia coupe Type 34
Valid as of June 11, 1961
Architecture
Rear-mounted engine, rear-wheel drive. Fuel tank and spare wheel between front wheels. Luggage space between front wheels, behind seats and above engine compartment.

Dimensions

Wheelbase	2400 mm	94.5 in.
Track, front	1310 mm	51.2 in.
Track, rear	1346 mm	53.0 in.
Overall length	4280 mm	168.5 in.
Overall width	1620 mm	63.8 in.
Overall height (unladen)	1335 mm	52.6 in.
Ground clearance	138 mm	5.4 in.
Minimum turn diameter	10.7 m	35.1 ft.

Weight

Dry weight	910 kg	2006 lb.
Payload capacity	400 kg	882 lb.
Maximum all-up weight	1310 kg	2889 lb.
Maximum front end load	550 kg	1213 lb.
Maximum rear end load	790 kg	1742 lb.

Engine

Layout		Horizontally opposed four-cylinder with individual finned cylinder barrels screwed into a common crankcase.
Cooling		Forced air: shrouded fan mounted on a vertical shaft above the cylinders, driven by helical gears.
Bore	83.0 mm	3.27 in.
Stroke	69.0 mm	2.72 in.
Displacement	1493 cc	91.1 cu.in.
Compression ratio	8.5:1	
Carburetor	2 Solex downdraft 32 PDSIT	
Valves	Overhead, inclined at 9° from the cylinder axis, operated by pushrods and rocker arms.	

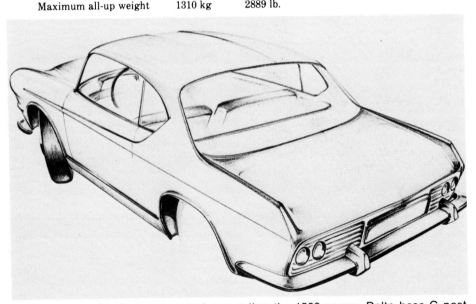

One of Sartorelli's last proposals for restyling the 1500 coupe. Delta-base C-post and stubby tailfins stopped it before a model was made.

116

Valve timing	Inlet opens 7°30′ BTC
	Inlet closes 37° ABC
	Exhaust opens 44°30′ BBC
	Exhaust closes 4° ATC
Camshaft	Located directly below the crankshaft and driven by spur gears. Cast iron with integral cams.
Crankshaft	One-plane forged steel, counterweighted running in 4 main bearings.
Connecting rods	Forged steel, I-beam profile
Pistons	Cast aluminum with steel insert
Maximum output	54 hp DIN @ 4200 rpm, 66 hp SAE gross @ 4800 rpm
Maximum torque	10.8 m-kg @ 2400 rpm, 83 lb.ft. SAE gross @ 3000 rpm

Drive train

Clutch	Single dry plate
Transmission	4-speed manual gearbox, synchromesh on all forward speeds.
Gear ratios	1st, 3.80:1; 2nd, 2.06; 3rd, 1.32; 4th, 0.89; Rev, 3.88.

Final drive	Spiral bevel
Final drive ratio	4.125:1

Chassis

Front suspension	Dual trailing links (upper and lower) per wheel, with transverse torsion bars, stabilizer bar and telescopic shock absorbers.
Rear suspension	Pendulum-type swing axles with trailing arms, transverse torsion bars, transverse camber-compensating bar and telescopic shock absorbers.
Steering	Worm-and-roller, with hydraulic damper on the steering linkage.
Steering gear ratio	18.5:1
Overall steering ratio	14.9:1
Turns lock-to-lock	2.8
Maximum steering angle	27° (outside wheel), 30° (inside wheel)
Steering wheel diameter	400 mm 15.75 in.
Brakes	Four-wheel hydraulic w/o power assist, dual hydraulic

Wooden workbench model made by Coggiola for the Karmann-Ghia coupe 1500 prototype.

Karmann built prototypes of a Type 34 convertible, but it was never accepted for production.

To many, the 1500 Karmann-Ghia cabriolet looked better than the coupe.

	circuits, split between front and rear. Drums front and rear, duo-servo shoes at front end.		
Drum diameter	248 mm	9.8 in.	
Lining area	960 cm²		
Wheels and tires	Tire size	6.00 S 15 L	
	Rim size	4½J-15	
Dynamic roll radius	309 mm	12.2 in.	
Inflation pressure	1.1 Bar (front) 16 psi, 1.7 Bar (rear) 25 psi.		

Performance

Top speed	132 km/h 82.5 mph
Acceleration	0-50 km/h (31 mph) 4.5 sec.
	0-60 km/h (37 mph) 7.2 sec.
	0-80 km/h (50 mph) 14.8 sec.
	0-100 km/h (62 mph) 22.0 sec.
Fuel consumption	(DIN calculated average 70030) 8.6 liters per 100 km (27.3 mpg)
Hill-climbing ability	1st gear, 45% gradient; 2nd, 24%; 3rd, 14%; 4th, 8%.

Two important technical innovations were made in 1967: A fully automatic transmission became optional on all Type 3 Volkswagens, and all U.S. versions of the VW 1600 were equipped with Bosch electronic fuel injection. Contrary to expectations, neither did much to increase the popularity of the Type 34 coupe or the Type 31 four-passenger convertible. Production of the Karmann-Ghia coupe came to an end in June 1969, after a total of 42,432 had been built.

Cockpit of the fastback Type 34 prototype had production-model interior.

A further variation on instrument panels appeared on the Type 34 convertible.

A further Sartorelli idea for eliminating the curlicues on the front panel, from about 1963.

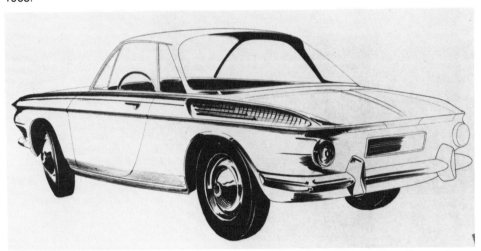

Facelift for the Type 34 rear end, with stylized air intakes in the fenders. Drawn by Sartorelli, about 1963.

Type 34 profile shows excellent proportions, with front and rear overhang kept within reasonable limits.

Chapter Six

THE SEARCH FOR AND REALIZATION OF THE NEW GENERATION VW

The longer Nordhoff waited before finding a true and popular successor to the Beetle, the greater the changes would have to be. Type 3 turned out to be no alternative at all, and in the final count, its sales were disappointing.

During 1963 Nordhoff was negotiating with Swiss engineer Hermann Klaue about Klaue's coming to Wolfsburg as chief of car design and development. Klaue posed the condition that his first task should be the replacement of the Beetle by a new front-wheel-drive car. The Klaue design, submitted in several stages in March and April 1963, showed a transversely mounted water-cooled four-cylinder engine of 1500 cc displacement.

But Nordhoff was not mentally prepared for such a drastic change. He shelved the Klaue proposal. Instead, he promoted Helmut Orlich to chief engineer for new-model development, which meant that his main duties were to explain Volkswagen's needs to Porsche, and to correctly assess the proposals offered by the Zuffenhausen establishment.

Under Nordhoff's guidance (heavily marketing oriented) and Orlich's direction, Porsche and VW developed a new four-door sedan, Type 411, with a chassis that seemed up-scale from the Super-Beetle and a body that looked like a taxicab version of the VW 1600 TL fastback. It went into production in 1968 and ran into a wall of resistance in the market place.

The failure of the VW 411 was due to the fact that its creators turned their backs on what the competition was doing: Renault followed the R-16 with the R-12; Fiat used the Autobianchi Primula as a guinea pig for changing the whole product line to front-wheel drive; and after the 204 success, Peugeot branched out into 304 and 104 models with the same architecture.

VW had spent over $50 million on designing, preparing and tooling for the 411. Production was planned for 800 per day. But the car failed to attract customers, and production was soon trimmed to 200 a day. The only reason the 411 was not discontinued right away was that Volkswagen was locked into certain supplier contracts for components that could not be used on other models.

The 411 had been his pet project, but Heinz Nordhoff did not live to suffer its defeat. He died on April 12, 1968. For Volkswagen, his sudden disappearance changed everything. In the legacy he left for his successors was a majority stake in Auto Union, makers of the Audi car in Ingolstadt.

Post-Nordhoff management.

One of the things Heinz Nordhoff had neglected was to provide for his succession. There was no crown prince of Wolfsburg, no one who was being groomed for the top job. The VW management board had to look outside for new talent, and that meant talent with experience of running a big industrial outfit. They picked a man named Kurt Lotz.

Kurt Lotz was born on September 18, 1912, in Lenderscheid near Ziegenhain as one of nine children in a farmer's family. He was educated at the August Vilmar High School in Homberg and entered police service through competitive examinations in 1932. He rose rapidly through the ranks and received a promotion to lieutenant in 1934. Going into military service in 1935, he served as an officer on the Luftwaffe's general staff from 1942 until 1945. Assigned to organizational and economic matters, he held the rank of major at the end of World War II.

It was in April 1946 that Lotz joined the great engineering firm of Brown, Boveri & Cie at Dortmund as a $75-a-month cost accountant. He studied industrial management at Dortmund's evening college. In 1947 he was transferred to the firm's German headquarters in Mannheim, working on cost accounting and cost control assignments. Then he was invited to join the company's central industrial management division, which was responsible for planning and budgeting for the entire corporation.

In 1954 Lotz was named head of Brown, Boveri & Cie's business division. Within three years he was appointed to the German subsidiary's management board, and in 1958 he was elected chairman. In 1961 he became a director of the parent firm, Brown, Boveri & Cie of Baden, Switzerland, and was elected managing director in 1963. The Institute of Economics in Mannheim awarded Lotz an honorary doctorate of political economics in 1963 in recognition of his work in industrial management, particularly in the fields of planning, organization and personnel management.

Clearly, without any automotive experience, Lotz's fate at the head of Volkswagen would greatly depend on the men he picked as his product planners and designers. His first key appointment was that of Werner Holste as technical director of Volkswagen on October 1, 1968. Born in Westfalen, Werner Holste was then just thirty years old. He had studied heat engines and machinery at the Technical University of Aachen (Aix-la-Chapelle), then went to Demag in Duisburg and became chief of the construction-equipment engineering department.

Heirloom from Neckarsulm: NSU K-70 in the foreground, with the Ro-80 behind and above.

He also started negotiations to get control of a small producer of technically exquisite cars in Neckarsulm, some forty miles north of Stuttgart: NSU Motorenwerke. NSU was co-licensor for the Wankel engine, and built a range of small cars with rear-mounted (transverse) air-cooled engines as well as a mid-size front-wheel-drive car in the BMW-Mercedes price class: Ro-80. The acquisition papers were signed in February 1969.

But there were other reasons why Lotz wanted NSU, and one of the most powerful was the existence of the NSU company's new K70 model, a medium-size front-wheel-drive car powered by a conventional 1.7-liter water-cooled, four-cylinder engine. This was a car built along Audi lines as opposed to VW lines and seemed a logical replacement for the unsuccessful VW 411 and a promising starting point for a new generation of VW economy cars with front-wheel drive.

Strangely, the K70 was killed on the eve of its introduction as an NSU product, but was revived in July 1970 as a VW model. Production had been transferred from Neckarsulm to Salzgitter, where it was scheduled for a rate of 500 cars a day.

Lotz was also preparing to relinquish the old, established contract with Porsche. Early in 1970 Lotz had given instructions to Werner Holste and Hans Georg Wenderoth (transferred from NSU) to go to work on a front-wheel-drive Beetle successor with a water-cooled engine.

Before Lotz's arrival, research and development was a very modest activity at Wolfsburg, but Lotz took steps to increase the technical staff and budget tenfold.

Concurrently, down at Ingolstadt, Audi's chief engineer, Ludwig Kraus, was busy with a new project that became the Audi 80. It is impossible that Lotz could have been ignorant of this, but it is true that he had a bewildering profusion of different cars, actual and potential, to sort out.

In addition to the Audi and NSU creations, the projects under study at Wolfsburg and fresh ideas from Karmann and Giugiaro's Ital Design studio (which Lotz began to consult when Ghia fell into the Ford camp), there was the flow of new proposals from Porsche.

Considering only the car in current production, it would not be possible to coordinate it with the existing VW range and rationalize engine production, body fabrication, and final assembly on any sort of profitable basis. Uppermost in Lotz's mind was the Beetle successor, and that's where Porsche threw in its resources to considerable effect.

The best known of the Porsche proposals was the EA 266, conceived about 1968, and still being tested in mid-1970. It was a break with tradition in several ways, for it had a water-cooled in-line four-cylinder pancake engine, mounted transversely under the back seat. Mechanically sound, this engine position had the disadvantage of pushing up the back seat and therefore raising the roofline (due to rear headroom requirements), heating up the back seat and making service and maintenance work on the engine pretty difficult.

VW four-wheel-drive Iltis was derived from the Passat. It was first developed as a military vehicle. The civilian version appeared in 1979.

A second version of the EA 266 had the same pancake engine offset to the right, mounted with its crankshaft in the direction of the car's center line and driving a transaxle extending straight backward.

But Werner Holste opposed these Porsche projects, not simply to favor his own, for in all fairness, it must be said that he seemed ready to try anything if it made industrial and commercial sense.

One Holste-sponsored project, the EA 276 from May 1969, was a boxy front-wheel-drive car with a Beetle engine mounted ahead of the front wheel axis. It had MacPherson front suspension and an independent rear end with trailing links and torsion bars.

With the EA 272 of 1970, Holste and Wenderoth came pretty close to the final Golf configuration, with a water-cooled in-line four-cylinder engine mounted transversely and driving the front wheels.

At the time, however, VW and Audi were independently working on new 1.5-liter engines. By Lotz's decision, the VW engine project was shelved in favor of the Audi Type 827 engine for the 80. The rest of the EA 272 was also shelved to concentrate all resources on the Audi 80 (Fox) and its VW-labeled derivative, the Passat (Dasher).

By that decision, Lotz made it necessary to use a version (or several) of the Audi 827 engine also in the Beetle successor. The big difference was that while it was mounted longitudinally and slanted to the right in the Passat, it was mounted transversely and slanted backward in the Golf.

While Lotz was doing his level best to turn the company around, and Holste with his lieutenants were making intelligent product-renewal decisions, time ran out on them. Volkswagen was losing market share, profits turned to deficits and the management board decided to back other horses.

On September 24, 1971, Kurt Lotz resigned, and the board invited Rudolf Leiding, president of Audi, to take the reins in Wolfsburg. He arrived on October 1, 1971, bringing with him his technical chief, Ludwig Kraus. Werner Holste and the vice president in charge of sales, Carl Hahn, left shortly afterward.

"Lotz of trouble," they had called him. But VW's troubles were far from over. At that time, the Salzgitter plant was building 387 K-70's a day; the Wolfsburg plant was making the Type 3 at a rate of 1,088 a day; and daily output of the 411 had been brought up to about 500. About 5,000 Beetles a day rolled off the lines at Wolfsburg and Emden.

The Audi 80 made its debut in July 1972, followed by the Passat in May 1973. That was just the beginning of an industrial revolution that has never had its like in European automotive history for sheer audacity and speed. Leiding was to Wolfsburg what Patton was to World War II. By the end of 1973, Passat production had reached a rate of 1,320 cars a day.

At the age of fifty-seven, Rudolf Leiding was a twenty-six-year VW veteran who had a terrific track record as a production engineer in various German plants, and as boss of VW do Brasil from 1968 to 1971.

Ludwig Kraus came from Mercedes-Benz, where he had worked on racing cars, production-car engines, and chassis. He developed an interest in front-wheel drive, and tried to get the company to build some test cars.

Instead, Mercedes-Benz bought control of Auto Union, and in 1963 Kraus was delegated to Ingolstadt as director of DKW engineering. In creating the F-12 and F-102, he did away with the two-stroke engines and put in new four-stroke units of his own design. The name of the car was changed from DKW to Audi, and in 1965-66, Mercedes-Benz sold the company to Volkswagen. Now, at Wolfsburg, Leiding told him to come up with a range of "Krausmobiles."

Kraus and Leiding decided on a new strategy for replacing the Beetle: not one but two successors—one at the low end (Polo) and one at the high end (Golf/Rabbit). By going to a modular product range, instead of using different bodies on a variety of chassis versions, costs could be controlled better, and productivity improved by a wide margin.

Volkswagen was changing the product in four fundamental ways:

1. From rear-wheel drive with a rear engine to front-wheel drive (some models with a transverse engine).
2. From air-cooled flat-four engines to water-cooled in-line engines.
3. From bodies with separate backbone-and-platform frames to unit-construction body shells.
4. From a double-jointed rear axle to a simple torsion-beam spindle carrier, and from a front axle assembly with either torsion-bar or coil spring units to a new system with MacPherson spring legs.

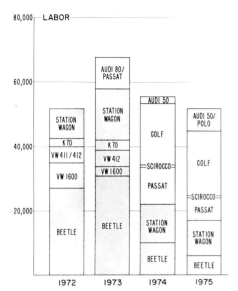

The number of workers assigned to Beetle production was cut by two thirds from 1973 to 1974, to make way for the Golf.

This list shows the scope of the necessary retooling. But that's not all. Type 1 body assembly had been fully automated, so that fifty-five workers could produce 2,600 body shells a day. With the new models, due to the lower production volume of each, automation would not be economically feasible. Instead, a manual setup was used, which enabled 182 workers to complete 1,000 body shells a day. The new equipment was acquired at a cost of $3.85 million, for the $13.5 million automated line had become obsolete.

Another great problem was the need to avoid disruption in the production of current models while tooling up for new ones. In the components plants, such as Kassel for transmissions and Braunschweig for front suspension assemblies, new production lines had to be set up alongside operating plants. It was only in Salzgitter that new engine lines could be installed with ease.

When you keep in mind that the machine tool industry works with delivery times of six to eighteen months, the speed of the plant conversions

Volkswagen Type 181 was developed in Germany but produced in Mexico. It was a recreational vehicle based on the Type 1 chassis, with a body inspired by the wartime Kübelwagen. Production began in 1969.

becomes even more impressive. Under normal circumstances, VW's own staff would have designed and built eighty percent of the press tools and other production equipment needed for a new model. But due to the high number of models involved and the tight timetable, VW was able to cope with only thirty-five percent of this work itself. The remaining sixty-five percent of new tools and equipment was placed on order with 350 suppliers all over the world.

Final assembly methods also had to be changed. Types 1 and 3 could be assembled on conveyor belts because of their separate body and frame construction, while the new unit-construction bodies had to be carried at a convenient height by overhead conveyors. This was expensive, but it also led to vastly improved working conditions on the line.

A successor for the Karmann-Ghia.

Kraus saw it as fairly simple to develop a sports coupe from the Golf/Rabbit sedan. In fact, the Golf and the Scirocco were developed side by side, and the Scirocco was actually introduced first.

Concurrently, Leiding was chopping obsolete cars from the program, right, left and center. Born in 1912, Kraus became eligible for retirement in 1973, and left Volkswagen. Ernst Fiala then became technical director for Volkswagen.

The old generation, 1972-73.

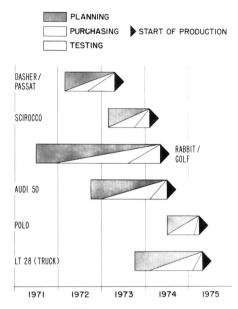

LEAD TIMES NEW MODELS

From mid-1971 to early 1975, 6 new vehicles were developed and put on the market. Delivery time for new tools and machinery varied from 6 to 18 months.

Ernst Fiala was the brain behind the VW experimental safety vehicles. He became technical director of Volkswagen when Ludwig Kraus retired.

Austrian by birth, Fiala had come to Volkswagen at age forty-two as research chief in 1970. He had studied mechanical engineering and got his degree after two years' postgraduate work under Professor Richter at the Institute for Combustion Engines and Motor Vehicles in Vienna.

He went to Mercedes-Benz in 1954 as a test engineer and stayed there for nine years. When he left he was chief of the body test department. In 1963 he went to Berlin to lecture at the Motor Vehicle Institute of the local university, and played a prominent part in auto-engineering discussions.

However, Fiala had little direct influence on the Scirocco and Golf that went into production in 1974. The chief engineer was Hermann Hablitzel. Body engineering was entrusted to Ch. Hildebrandt, and testing and development to Friedrich Goes.

Introduction of the Passat coincided with the shutdown of the Type 3 production line at Wolfsburg, and the transfer of Type 4 production to the Salzgitter plant. In September 1973 the Brussels plant lowered its Beetle output and began producing the Passat/Dasher. In November 1973, some Passat-building capacity was transferred from Wolfsbürg to Salzgitter, to make way for the Golf and Scirocco.

Production of the air-cooled engines had been moved to the Hanover plant on November 1, 1958. All the new water-cooled engines were made at the Salzgitter plant, which Lotz had built for some $150 million. Production of parts for the Scirocco began at Salzgitter and Wolfsburg in February 1974, with assembly by Karmann at Osnabrück.

Karmann also assembled the Porsche 914, starting in October 1969. It was widely believed that the 914/4, a roadster with a midships-mounted air-cooled flat-four VW engine, was intended as a replacement for the Karmann-Ghia, but neither Volkswagen nor Karmann saw it that way. The concept was too different, they were not competing in the same price range and the timing would have been all wrong, for the Karmann-Ghia was at the peak of its popularity when the 914 was launched. No, the true successor of the Karmann-Ghia was the Scirocco, with a production overlap of only about four months.

Production of the 1200 Beetle was taken out of the Wolfsburg plant in March 1974, and moved to Hanover.

Golf production began at Wolfsburg in April 1974 and hit a peak of 2,000 units a day in October/November. The Emden plant, built in 1964 at a cost of $65 million, and specially equipped to build Type 1 cars for the U.S. market, was also retooled for Golf production.

DAILY VEHICLE PRODUCTION RATE				
PLANT	*PRODUCT*	*End 1973*	*End 1974*	*Projected end 1975*
Wolfsburg	Type 1	2,000	---	---
	Passat	1,430	270	270
	Golf	---	1,500	2,000
	Polo/Audi 50	---	500	1,100
Hanover	LT-28	---	---	750
	Type 2	920	774	220
Emden	Type 1	1,160	340	---
	Golf	---	560	1,000
Salzgitter	K-70	90	60	---
	Type 4	264	---	---
	Passat	30	380	450
Brussels	Type 1	430	240	90
	Passat	100	200	300
Total		6,424	4,824	6,180

In the meantime, Kraus had come up with a still smaller car, the Audi 50, which went into production at Wolfsburg in June 1974. In July, assembly of Type 1303 (Super-Beetle) was transferred to Emden, and the Wolfsburg plant was no longer building the car for which it had originally been created.

Also in July 1974, VW 412 production came to an end at Salzgitter. And the K-70, which had never proved profitable to VW, was discontinued in February 1975.

Volkswagen got its sister model to the Audi 50, called Polo, into production in March 1975, in the Wolfsburg plant. Output of the two models was soon running at the level of 900 a day.

Plans for the Polo existed as early as 1970. It was developed in the 1970-73 period, under code name EA 337, with a forward tilt on its transverse engine, which was a new and smaller design than the Audi 827.

The car that became the VW Scirocco started out as a project with the code number EA 398. It was to share a maximum of mechanical components with the Golf, and even the floor and many body parts were to be

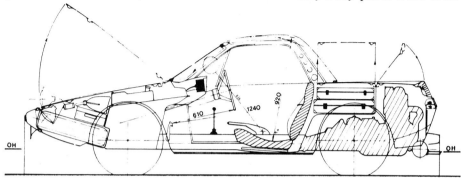

This drawing shows how Giugiaro was able to fit a modern wedge-style body on the VW Type 1 chassis.

VW Karmann Cheetah cabriolet of 1971 was the start of Ital Design's consulting work for Wolfsburg.

interchangeable. Both the Golf and the Scirocco were styled in Italy. The contract with Ital Design stemmed from the fact that Kurt Lotz went to the Turin motor show in 1969 and made a list of the best-looking small cars. He found that four out of six had been designed by Giugiaro. That led to contracts with Ital Design for the creation of styling packages for the new-generation VW cars.

Wilhelm Karmann, Jr., thought Giugiaro was the best choice, too, and stressed the coincidence that Giugiaro worked for Ghia from 1965 to 1968, as historical justification for the change.

Ital Design's first proposal for Lotz was the Karmann Cheetah, based on a regular Type 14 chassis, and exhibited at the Geneva auto show in March 1971. Karmann built the prototype, a two-seater hardtop convertible, and submitted it to Volkswagen.

Body structure in process of completion at the Karmann works.

Body shells after anticorrosion bath, ready for the paint shop.

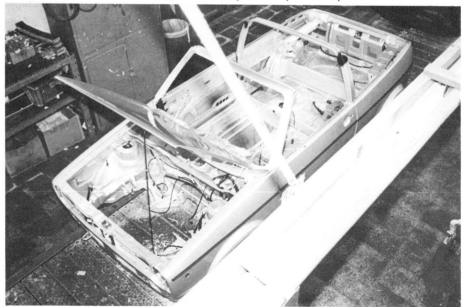

After painting, assembly begins by putting in the wiring harness.

Here was a fashionable wedge profile, a resilient plastic bumper, concealed headlights and obviously good aerodynamics, combined with sheet metal that was quite easy to press and weld into a coherent structure. But Volkswagen—perhaps mainly due to Lotz's mounting difficulties—showed no interest in it.

Karmann engineers claim that Ital Design did nothing more with it, but that Bertone's new designer, Marcello Gandini, was inspired to imitate it in the form of the Fiat X-1/9 roadster of 1972.

It is uncertain that the Cheetah did anything to help Giugiaro get the styling contracts for the Passat, Scirocco and Golf, but he did. One of his wilder prototypes, called Ace of Spades, using the Audi 80 chassis and shown publicly in 1973, probably had even less to do with it. Designs and scale models were delivered in record time, and were accepted.

Top goes on before the mechanical elements are added.

Karmann was contracted for body stampings, body shell welding, painting and final assembly of the Scirocco. But while Karmann was busy getting new tools and dies ready, practically all the body engineering was done at Wolfsburg. In the Scirocco program, Volkswagen was much more closely involved at the product end than had ever been the case with the Karmann-Ghia.

SPECIFICATIONS
Volkswagen Scirocco
Valid as of December 14, 1973
Architecture
Transversely mounted engine in the front, with front-wheel drive. Fuel tank below rear seat, spare wheel located below trunk floor. Luggage space in the tail, accessible through top-hinged hatch.
Dimensions

Wheelbase	2400 mm	94.5 in.
Track, front	1390 mm	54.7 in.
Track, rear	1350 mm	53.1 in.
Overall length	3845 mm	151.4 in.
Overall width	1625 mm	64.0 in.
Overall height (unladen)	1310 mm	51.6 in.
Ground clearance	125 mm	4.9 in.
Minimum turn diameter	9.8 m	32.2 ft.

Weight

Dry weight	775 kg	1709 lb.
Payload capacity	375 kg	827 lb.
Maximum all-up weight	1150 kg	2536 lb.

Engine installation and front suspension of the Scirocco.

Engines and chassis components are delivered to Karmann from VW plants, and mounted in the body shell at Osnabrück. Here's the production line.

Maximum front end load	590 kg	1300 lb.	
Maximum rear end load	560 kg	1235 lb.	

Engine

Layout	In-line four-cylinder with cast iron block and light alloy cylinder head.		
Cooling	Water, with radiator and mechanical water pump, electric fan with thermostatic control.		
L engine			
Bore	69.5 mm	2.74 in.	
Stroke	72.0 mm	2.83 in.	
Displacement	1093 cc	66.7 cu.in.	
Compression ratio	8.0:1		
S, LS, TS engines			
Bore	76.5 mm	3.01 in.	
Stroke	80.0 mm	3.15 in.	
Displacement	1471 cc	89.7 cu.in.	
Compression ratio	S, LS 8.2:1 TS 9.7:1		
Carburetor	L, S, LS: 1 Solex one-barrel downdraft 35 PICT - 5 TS: 1 Solex two-barrel downdraft 32/35 TDID		

Valves	Overhead, in line with cylinder axis, operated direct by mechanical lifters from a belt-driven overhead camshaft.
Crankshaft	Forged steel, counterweighted, running in 5 main bearings.
Output	Base model and L: 50 hp @ 6000 rpm S, SL and TS: 70 hp @ 5800 rpm LS and TS: 85 hp @ 5800 rpm
Torque	Base model and L: 73.6 Nm (54 lb.ft.) @ 3500 rpm S, SL and TS: 102 Nm (75.5 lb.ft.) @ 3000 rpm LS and TS: 110.5 Nm (81 lb.ft.) @ 4000 rpm

Drive train

Clutch	Single dry plate
Transmission	4-speed manual gearbox mounted in line with crankshaft, integrated with final drive unit.

The 1974 Scirocco. L models had rectangular headlamps; the TS models had dual quartz-halogen lamps.

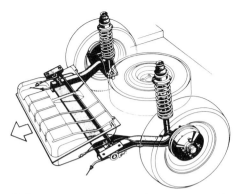

Scirocco rear suspension was semi-independent and incorporated a built-in stabilizer bar.

Gear ratios		L	S, LS	TS
	1	3.45	3.45	3.45
	2	2.05	1.96	1.96
	3	1.35	1.37	1.37
	4	0.96	0.97	0.97
	Rev	3.39	3.17	3.17

Final drive	Helical gears
Final drive ratio	L, 4.57:1; S, LS, 3.76:1, TS, 3.76:1.
Transmission	Optional on S, LS, TS: 3-speed fully automatic transmission, with hydraulic torque converter and planetary gears.
Gear ratios	1st, 2.55:1; 2nd, 1.45; 3rd, 1.00; Rev, 2.41.
Final drive ratio (with optional automatic)	3.76:1

Chassis

Front suspension	Lower A-arms, MacPherson spring legs with high-mounted

1978 Scirocco GTI with 110 hp fuel-injection engine.

	coil springs enclosing mono-tube shock absorbers.	
Rear suspension	Pressed steel axle beam with integral stabilizer bar, mounted on trailing arms, with vertical coil springs, telescopic shock absorbers.	
Steering	Rack-and-pinion	
Steering gear ratio	14.5:1	
Overall steering ratio	17.3:1	
Turns, lock-to-lock	3.25	
Brakes	Four-wheel hydraulic with dual circuits, split diagonally. Power assist by vacuum booster. Front discs with solid rotors, rear drums.	
Disc diameter	239 mm	9.4 in.
Drum diameter	180 mm	7.1 in.

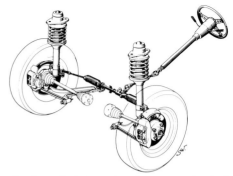

Rack-and-pinion steering was adopted for the Scirocco. Also seen here are front-wheel driveshafts and outboard-mounted disc brakes.

1979-model Scirocco had new light-alloy wheels as an option.

Lining width, rear	30 mm	1.2 in.
Lining area, front	105 cm²	16.3 sq.in.
Lining area, rear	189 cm²	29.3 sq.in.
Wheels and tires	Tire size	155 SR 13
	Optional	175/70 SR 13
	Rim size	5J-13
	Optional	5½J-13
Inflation pressure	2.0 Bar (front) 30 psi, 1.8 Bar (rear) 26 psi	

Performance

Top speed		
L	144 km/h	89.5 mph
S, LS	164 km/h	102.5 mph
TS	175 km/h	109 mph

Acceleration	L	S, LS	TS
0-50 km/h (31 mph)	6.0 sec.	4.5 sec.	3.8 sec.
0-60 km/h (37 mph)	8.1 sec.	6.2 sec.	5.6 sec.
0-80 km/h (50 mph)	13.2 sec.	9.4 sec.	8.8 sec.
0-100 km/h (62 mph)	18.0 sec.	12.5 sec.	11.0 sec.

Second-generation Scirocco was introduced at the Geneva auto show in March 1981. VW stylist Herbert Schäfer is credited with the design.

Many further varieties of Scirocco power trains were to come. The U.S. version had a 1588 cc engine with K-Jetronic and low compression (for regular fuel), while the same basic setup was turned into a GTI with high compression for European markets.

In Germany, the Scirocco trounced the Ford Capri and Opel Manta, with sales up to 4,000 cars a month in the years 1976-79. During that period, Volkswagen had expanded its own styling studio at Wolfsburg under Herbert Schäfer, to make proposals in open competition with Giugiaro's (as well as having the opportunity of "correcting" Giugiaro's). Schäfer was not in favor of the crisp lines of the Scirocco, with its sharp angularity, and wanted a new Scirocco with softened lines.

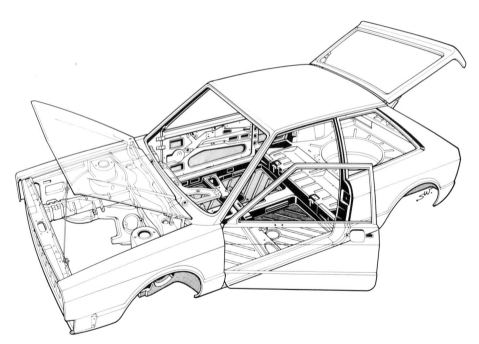

Unit-construction body for the Scirocco combined strength and light weight, without a separate frame. It had better trunk space than the Karmann-Ghia, plus a back seat.

What Giugiaro offered has not yet been released. But we know from some of Giugiaro's prototypes for other clients how his basic coupe shape evolved between 1973 and 1978.

In 1977 Ital Design presented the Ace of Diamonds, built by Karmann on a BMW 3-series chassis. Karmann was, of course, producing the bodies for the big BMW sports coupes, and would have liked to add a smaller companion model. But BMW, perhaps because of the too-close relationship to the Scirocco, did not want it.

Late in 1978, for the Turin auto show, Ital Design had a new car ready, the Ace of Clubs. The chassis was the Isuzu Gemini, with front engine and rear axle drive. Isuzu began building a production-model based directly on the Ace of Clubs in Japan in 1980, not long after Volkswagen had introduced its second-generation Scirocco, with styling credited entirely to Herbert Schäfer. Volkswagen's wind tunnel also played some part in it, for the aerodynamicists were able to find ways to cut the drag coefficient from 0.42 to 0.38.

Ace of Diamonds by Ital Design on a BMW 320 chassis foreshadowed the second-generation Scirocco. Giorgetto Giugiaro stands next to the car.

Ace of Clubs by Ital Design was built on an Isuzu Gemini chassis, and led to a Japanese production-model by Isuzu Motors.

The old and the new. The Golf convertible was introduced as a 1979 model, but Karmann actually built 18,511 before the end of 1978. Golf body structure was reinforced for convertible use. Doors had reinforcement ribs, floor had extra cross-members, and the rollover bar also contributed some stiffness.

Karmann's prototype Golf convertible. The production model followed four years behind the Golf sedan.

SPECIFICATIONS
Volkswagen Golf Convertible
Valid as of September 22, 1978
Architecture
Transversely mounted engine in the front, front-wheel drive. Fuel tank behind rear seat, spare wheel located below the trunk floor. Luggage space in tail, accessible through rear end panel.

Dimensions

Wheelbase		2400 mm	94.5 in.
Track, front	GLS	1390 mm	54.7 in.
	GLI	1404 mm	55.3 in.
Track, rear	GLS	1358 mm	53.5 in.
	GLI	1372 mm	54.0 in.
Overall length		3815 mm	150.2 in.
Overall width	GLS	1610 mm	63.4 in.
	GLI	1630 mm	64.2 in.
Overall height (unladen)	GLS	1410 mm	55.5 in.
	GLI	1395 mm	54.9 in.
Ground clearance		124 mm	4.9 in.
Minimum turn diameter		10.3 m	33.8 ft.

Weight

Dry weight	GLS	910 kg	2006 lb.
	GLI	940 kg	2072 lb.
Payload capacity		360 kg	794 lb.

Soft top folded completely away on Karmann's prototype. Volkswagen said it stole too much trunk space and ordered it put on the outside.

Top was weatherproof and heat-insulating. Profile was "faster" than on the sedan.

Maximum all-up height	1270 kg	2800 lb.
Maximum front end load	572 kg	1260 lb.
Maximum rear end load	698 kg	1540 lb.

Engine

Layout	In-line four-cylinder with cast iron block and light alloy cylinder head.	
Cooling	Water: radiator and mechanical pump, electric fan with thermostatic control.	
Bore	79.5 mm	3.13 in.
Stroke	GLS 73.4 mm	2.89 in.
	GLI 80 mm	3.15 in.
Displacement	GLS 1439 cc.	87.8 cu.in.
	GLI 1577 cc.	96.2 cu.in.
Compression ratio	GLS, 8.2:1; GLI, 9.5:1.	

Carburetor	GLS, 1 Solex 34 PICT-5; GLI, Bosch K-Jetronic fuel injection.
Valves	Overhead, in line with cylinder axis, operated direct by mechanical lifters from a belt-driven overhead camshaft.
Camshaft	Cast iron with integral cams, belt-driven from the crankshaft.
Maximum output	GLS, 70 hp DIN at 5600 rpm; GLI, 110 hp DIN at 6100 rpm
Maximum torque	GLS, 110 Nm at 2500 rpm; GLI, 140 Nm at 4000 rpm

Drivetrain

Clutch	Single dry plate

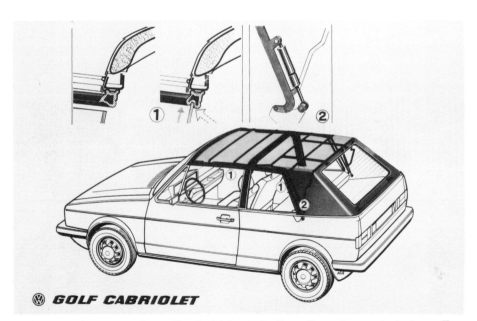

The mechanism was scissor-like, held firmly to the rollover bar and windows. Two sturdy clips fastened it to the windshield frame, and two gas-filled springs aided in handling the top.

Transmission	Standard: 4-speed manual gearbox mounted in line with crankshaft
Gear ratios	1st, 3.45:1; 2nd, 1.94; 3rd, 1.37; 4th, 0.97; Rev, 3.17.
Final drive	Helical gears
Final drive ratio	3.90:1
Optional on GLS	3-speed fully automatic transmission, with hydraulic torque converter and planetary gearing.

Chassis

Front suspension	MacPherson spring legs with high-mounted coil springs, enclosing monotube shock absorbers.
Rear suspension	Pressed-steel axle beam with integral stabilizer bar, mounted on trailing arms, with vertical coil springs, telescopic shock absorbers.
Steering	Rack-and-pinion
Overall steering ratio	20.8:1
Turns, lock-to-lock	3.9
Brakes	Four-wheel hydraulic with dual circuits, split diagonally, vacuum booster. Front discs with solid rotors, rear drums.
Disc diameter	239 mm 9.4 in.
Drum diameter	180 mm 7.1 in.
Lining width	30 mm 1.2 in.
Lining area	105 cm², 16.3 sq.in. (front); 189 cm², 29.3 sq.in. (rear)
Tire size	GLS, 155 SR 13; GLI, 175/70 SR 13.
Rim size	GLS, 5J 13; GLI, 5½ J 13.
Inflation pressure	2.0 (front) 30 psi, 1.8-2.2 (rear) 26-32 psi.

Folding the top was a one-person operation. The heated rear window fit into the folds. Note B-post combined into rollover bar.

Performance

Top speed	GLS, 150 km/h, 93 mph; GLI, 172 km/h, 107 mph.	
Acceleration	GLS	GLI
0-50 km/h (31 mph)	5.0 sec.	3.3 sec.
0-60 km/h (37 mph)	6.6 sec.	4.4 sec.
0-80 km/h (50 mph)	10.7 sec.	7.2 sec.
0-100 km/h (62 mph)	14.3 sec.	10.2 sec.

The U.S. version was a hybrid, using the 1588 cc (97 cu. in.) block, with a low 8.2:1 compression ratio to permit the use of unleaded gasoline. Fuel was injected (K-Jetronic), and a three-way catalytic converter was fitted on the exhaust pipe. It was rated at 76 hp at 5500 rpm, with a peak torque of 83 lb.ft. (113 Nm or 11.5 m-kg) at 3200 rpm. It took fourteen seconds for the 0-60 mph acceleration run, and had a top speed of 95 mph, with an average fuel mileage of 27 mpg (according to *Road & Track*).

VW Auto 2000.

What will be the next generation of VW-Karmann sports cars? Some clues as to the possible shape and engineering content are given by the VW

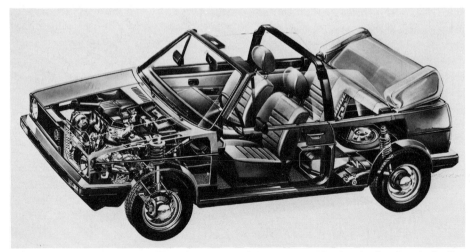

No trunk space was lost to the soft top when folded down. Mechanically, the similarity between the Golf and the Scirocco was obvious.

Auto 2000, built in 1981 under a government research contract. Volkswagen's research chief, Dr. Ulrich Seiffert, and the chief engineer, Dr. Wolfgang Lincke, make no secret of the fact that it is serving as a rolling laboratory for ideas they intend to use in future production cars.

What reveals most, however, about VW's real future product plans is the thinking that went into the Auto 2000. Particular thought was given to production technology and assembly processes. The job environment was given strong emphasis. Repairs had to be simple and easy. Recycling of materials was kept in mind throughout.

The VW 2000 started not as a stylist's concept, but in the wind tunnel. A suggested ideal body form created in 1922 by W. Klemperer at the Zeppelin works was found to have a drag coefficient of 0.15. The aerodynamicists at VW shortened it to fit the Golf wheelbase, and honed it till its C_x was no more than 0.16.

The VW Auto 2000 was built in 1981 under a government research contract. It will never go into production, but elements of its design and engineering will be used on future models.

Next, it was redesigned as a car, but the shape did not comply with legal requirements. Moreover, the available space under the hood was not suitable for engine installation. Adapting the basic shape to overcome these objections took a lot of time and wind tunnel work, but led to a basic model of a fully practical car with a drag coefficient of 0.24. The test car gave a reading of 0.25.

The body shape is extremely important for overall fuel economy, due to its effect on airflow. "Safety requirements may conflict with good aerodynamics," said Rolf Buchheim, chief of wind tunnel testing at VW, adding, "and production cost is a big problem."

Total air drag is the product of the frontal area and the drag coefficient. "When you start with the Golf as your base, frontal area is not reducible," he feels. Consequently, the drag coefficient (0.42 for the Golf) must be lowered. How much can it be lowered? "Thirty percent drag coefficient reduction is possible with a variety of shapes and fully practical bodies," was his hopeful answer.

Controls and instrument panel of the VW Auto 2000. Electronics played a big part in information and monitoring systems.

The VW 2000 is a two-door, four-passenger sedan built on the Golf's 94.5-inch wheelbase, with closely similar overall dimensions, but is 120-160 pounds lighter.

Great concern for lightness is evident throughout the car. The basic approach was to reduce surface area without loss of interior volume (including trunk space). Today's average VW has a surface/volume ratio of forty-five percent, and the goal is fifty-seven percent.

A secondary approach is material substitution, which comes down to using light alloys or plastics in place of steel. The opportunities for such substitutions in the body are obvious, and VW is not alone in experimenting with plastic for door panels, hoods, trunk lids, roof panels, wheel arches and other unstressed parts, as well as in bumper systems. But VW engineers are also looking at making chassis parts from lightweight materials. The fuel tank, for instance, can be made from plastics (as has been common on racing cars since the mid-sixties).

"We can make the whole rear axle in plastic," said a VW structure expert, "but it means a total redesign. It will no longer look the same, and such redesign will affect its attachments, and other parts in the same area. It goes through the whole car."

Once a satisfactory plastic rear axle has been developed, the same techniques can be carried over to other parts. How important can material

The body was designed for aerodynamics and not for practicality. But for a sports coupe, its lines might be a good starting point.

substitution become? A seventeen-percent weight reduction in the body and chassis of the production-model Golf is a realistic target, according to VW.

That would mean lowering the steel content in the total car from sixty-nine to fifty percent and raising the plastics content from ten to eighteen percent. Simultaneously, the aluminum content would go from three to eleven percent.

No one has realized better than Dr. Ulrich Seiffert that many key factors bound to influence future auto markets are outside the car makers' control. Factors such as fuel prices, sources and availability, motor vehicle legislation and taxation, roadbuilding plans and public-transit policies will have a bearing on trends in consumer preferences, particularly with regard to the balance between performance and fuel economy.

To be ready for all eventualities, the VW research department has prepared several different power trains corresponding to a number of scenarios. One is aimed at a market in which gasoline supplies are unrestricted and the rise in fuel prices has been contained. It's an economy car with the accent on performance. It has a supercharged gasoline engine.

A second one is matched to a darker picture, with petroleum-based motor fuels in short supply, at prices driven up and up by the producers, taxation, inflation and so on. It has a direct-injection turbocharged diesel engine. Both engines are based on existing production units.

Gasoline engine.

It is a modified 1050 cc Polo/Derby engine. Its main characteristics are oversquare dimensions (75 x 59 mm or 2.95 x 2.32 in.), belt-driven overhead camshaft, parallel valves and an ability to burn regular gasoline with a 9.5:1 compression ratio. The block is cast iron, the cylinder head aluminum, and the crankshaft runs in five main bearings.

The small displacement was chosen to maximize the time it's operating with high mean effective pressures (lowest specific fuel consumption). That gives the best fuel economy in urban driving, but the engine does not have enough torque to meet the acceleration target.

That's why the supercharger was installed. That solution also has further advantages. The blown engine delivers maximum power with lower friction losses, and runs more economically in part-load operation. For small-volume series, production costs may be lower than for a bigger engine.

Exhaustive testing was undertaken with turbochargers versus mechanically driven blowers, with cylinder heads giving an 8.3:1 compression ratio. A Roots-type blower, developed jointly with Aerzener Maschinenfabrik, was compared with Garrett T-2, KKK K-14 and Hitachi HT-10 turbochargers. The throttle-response lag of all turbochargers gave an advantage to the Roots blower. To add to its advantage, VW engineers rigged up a variable-speed blower drive, giving a 1:2.20 ratio at low crankshaft speeds (where maximum boost was needed), changing progressively to a

One of the engines tested in the VW Auto 2000 was a four-cylinder gasoline unit with variable-drive supercharger.

1:1.23 ratio in the 3000 rpm area (reducing blower-drive power consumption). This clever device consists of a belt-driven CVT (continuously variable transmission) with a magnetic clutch and a centrifugal governor. The magnetic clutch disengages the blower drive except for acceleration, so that under most conditions, it is inactive and consumes no power.

The Roots blower pumps up to 0.73 liters (44.5 cu.in.) per revolution at a pressure up to 1.5 Bar (22 psi). The engine delivers 75 hp DIN at 5700 rpm, with a maximum torque of 10.8 m-kg (76 lb.ft.) at 4000 rpm, for a weight of 150 kg (331 lb.). The standard 1050 cc engine weighs 140 kg (309 lb.) and delivers a maximum torque of 73 Nm (54 lb.ft.) at 2700 rpm.

While the production version has a Solex carburetor and a conventional ignition system, the experimental unit is fitted with Bosch L-Jetronic fuel injection (using a novel type of injector nozzle with smaller diameter) and an electronic ignition system whose advance curve is modified by a knock detector.

The spark is not retarded at the first "ping," however. Only sustained detonation will do that. And then begins a new, immediate but tentative spark advance, so that the engine is continuously running on the verge of knocking. That's what squeezes the most energy out of the fuel.

Several transmissions are under study for possible matching with this engine. The prototype was fitted with a standard VW three-speed automatic transmission. "The next one will have a four-speed automatic with a lockup clutch," stated Hans-Wilhelm Grove, project manager for the Auto 2000. Volkswagen is also considering the Van Doorne (stepless drive) Transmatic, and such units have been undergoing laboratory tests in preparation for in-car testing since 1980.

Added to the transmission in the test car is a free-wheel, which allows the engine to drop to idle speed whenever the accelerator pedal is released. The ignition and fuel-metering systems are set to assure low idle speed (650 rpm) which keeps idle consumption down to 0.5 liter (one pint) per hour.

Hans-Wilhelm Grove let me drive the test cars when I visited Wolfsburg in the summer of 1982. The gasoline-fueled car had outstanding performance. A lag in response, when starting off, or when suddenly stepping on the gas to speed up, was more due to slip in the hydraulic torque converter than to any flaw in the engine.

The shift pattern was not optimized for economy—automatic upshifts were timed for best acceleration. Zero-to-100 km/h (62 mph) acceleration took twelve seconds. As for top speed, we saw 185 km/h (115 mph) indicated before traffic forced us to slow down, but the car was still gaining speed and could probably have reached 190 km/h (118 mph).

Fuel economy? "At this speed, you are burning eight liters per 100 kilometers," said Hans-Wilhelm Grove, as I was driving along the Autobahn at a steady 160-161-162 km/h (100 mph, give or take a fraction). That corresponds to 29.6 mpg.

At a steady 120 km/h (74.5 mph), the fuel consumption is 5.6 liters per 100 km (42 mpg), and at 90 km/h (56 mph), it drops to 4.3 liters per 100 km (54.7 mph).

Turbo-Diesel engine.

The diesel engine represents three cylinders of the 1600 Golf GLD four-cylinder unit, with an aluminum block and a new 120-degree crankshaft with a 76.5 mm (3.01 inches) bore and an 86.4 mm (3.40 inches) stroke, the displacement is 1191 cc (72.7 cu.in.).

Three normal-size cylinders were chosen in preference to four smaller ones because of lower internal friction and reduced pumping losses. Direct fuel injection was chosen instead of the swirl-chamber design of the Golf GLD in combination with an experimental electronically controlled injection pump by Bosch. VW engine specialist Erich Gaschler says that direct injection gives ten to fifteen percent better fuel economy, because it avoids the heat rejection to the cylinder-head coolant and speeds the flame propagation. Here, the combustion chamber is contained in the piston crown, and has the shape of a bowl with a raised point at the center (Omega-bowl) so as to preserve the swirl generated in the airflow by the curved runners to the intake ports.

According to Volkswagen, the key to a successful direct-injection diesel engine lies in the injectors, and several types were tested.

These injector nozzles have three to five holes, with diameters from 0.15 to 0.25 mm (0.006 to 0.01 inch). That poses a severe production problem for the direct-injection diesel. At the same time, it demands an injection pump capable of delivering fuel with pressures above 500 Bar (7,350 psi) at the nozzle.

Cast iron cylinder liners are Nikasil-coated for a hard-wearing surface that's compatible with the aluminum pistons (whose rings have reduced prestress to minimize friction losses).

Because of the small displacement, some form of forced air induction was required. Here, the turbocharger was chosen in preference to the Roots blower and the Comprex pressure-wave supercharger. Output is 45 hp DIN at 4000 rpm, with a peak torque of 10.1 m-kg (72.7 lb.ft.) at 2500 rpm.

Another test engine used in the VW Auto 2000 was a three-cylinder direct-injection diesel with turbocharger and automatic stop/start device.

The diesel car is equipped with an automatic stop/start system and a manual four-speed gearbox with automatic clutch (no clutch pedal). Fuel supply is instantly cut when the accelerator is released, and the engine stops dead, at any speed, while the car free-wheels till the driver again accelerates. Restarting of the engine is done by a second flywheel and clutch, in response to accelerator movement. If flywheel speed should drop below 800 rpm when the engine is stopped, an electric motor speeds it up to 2000 rpm.

This system saves a considerable amount of fuel, since the engine is turned off during coasting, braking and stops. It has also eliminated the idle-noise problem!

The diesel car will not go beyond 150 km/h (93 mph) and needs twenty seconds for the 0-100 km/h (62 mph) acceleration run. But its fuel economy, on the other hand, is utterly sensational. At a constant 120 km/h (74.5 mph) it consumes 4.9 liters per 100 km (48 mpg). In the urban driving cycle (DIN 70030, which in contrast with the American LA-4 test cycle includes two idling periods), it does an ultra-frugal 4.2 liters per 100 km (56 mpg), and at a steady 90 km/h (56 mph) on the highway, it gives the amazing result of 3.3 liters per 100 km (71.2 mpg).

The very good high-speed fuel economy figures for both test cars are partly due to the extremely low aerodynamic drag of the Auto 2000.

The smart acceleration of the gasoline-fueled car reflects on the combination of electronic ignition with automatic spark advance controlled by signals from a knock sensor, and the variable-drive Roots compressor. And the exceptional performance of the diesel car in the urban driving cycle stems from the combination of a direct-injection diesel with an automatic stop/start system. These are some of the things you can expect in future Volkswagens.

Chapter Seven

THE KARMANN-GHIA IN AMERICA

by Richard M. Langworth

If the amount of interest taken in a product by its distributor is any gauge of its potential, the Karmann-Ghia didn't stand a chance. In 1956, the first year Karmann-Ghias were sold in the United States, only 2,452 found owners. Aside from a glossy sales brochure in stilted English, with radically inaccurate color illustrations, there was no media campaign, no advertising whatsoever. People were so busy buying Beetles, it seemed, they didn't even know what a Karmann-Ghia was.* In their first road test, the editors of *Road & Track* called the car a "Ghia-Karmann."

Though American Karmann-Ghia sales steadily improved, gaining about 2,000 units every year, Volkswagen of America still appeared to ignore its elegant two-seater. No Ghia advertisements appeared nationally until 1961. Then, however, the situation changed radically. A major Karmann-Ghia campaign was launched with an apology: "This ad is 6 years late." In 1962 for the first time, Ghia sales in America topped 10,000. They kept rising through 1966, when Volkswagen of America sold close to 22,000, and the best year on record was 1970, when no fewer than 38,825 Karmann-Ghias were registered. This was a staggering total for any car with as much hand workmanship as the Ghia contained.

The Ghia might have moved off to a much faster start had Volkswagen itself been better organized in the United States. But in its earliest years the Beetle had seemed to have no potential at all. The first two VWs

---

* VW's first big year was 1955, when it sold nearly 33,000 Beetles—the lion's share of a whopping sixty percent slice of the U.S. import market owned by West Germany. This was the first year that Germany supplanted Great Britain as the major source of imported cars in America.

This ad is 6 years late.

In the last 6 years this car has mystified millions.

People have called it everything from an Alfa Romeo to a Ferrari.

We've never advertised it in any national magazine before. You may have seen one on the road and wondered what it was.

Brace yourself.

It's a Volkswagen.

Our Karmann Ghia.

(We didn't mind its being Brand X. But we can't have people calling it by somebody else's name. The time has come to speak up.)

The Ghia is a limited production car. Only around nine thousand are made for this country each year.

It's because of the handwork that goes into the body.

We wouldn't even try to make it in the VW plant.

Most auto bodies are designed for an assembly line. One stamping per part. Thunk, a fender. Thunk, a door. Thunk, a hood.

The Ghia stopped us on the first thunk.

It was designed by Ghia of Turin, Italy, with lines that are too sculptured for mass production methods. The curve in the fender alone has to be made in 2 sections. Then welded together. Then shaped down by hand.

You can't stop and do this in a plant that's turning out 950,000 other cars.

So we turned to one of the most celebrated custom coachworks left in Europe, Karmann of Osnabruck. In the time it takes to mass produce three ordinary cars, Karmann makes one Ghia.

Inefficient? Of course. So was Cellini.

It takes over 185 men to make the Ghia body alone. That will give you an idea of the handwork that goes into it.

(You can't find a seam anywhere. Not even where the fenders join the hood. One lady said it looked as if it had been carved out of soap.)

But under its wanton exterior, the Ghia's all business.

Its lower center of gravity will hold a bumpy barreltop road at over 70—and take curves with aplomb if you're ever in a squeeze.

Best of all is the Volkswagen engine, transmission, suspension and chassis.

32 miles a gallon, regular gas, regular driving. (Some get a bit more, some a bit less.)

And a Volkswagen by any other name is just as sweet to service.

This is no temperamental prima donna that needs $40 monthly tuneups and $100 carburetors.

VW parts fit it and you can get them anywhere.

You also get VW's rear-engine traction in snow. And our air-cooling. (No water to freeze up or boil over. The Ghia keeps a cool head in the longest traffic jam.)

And VW's 40,000 miles on tires. And they almost never need balancing.

The Ghia also has the VW independent torsion bar suspension for all 4 wheels. When one hits a bump, it keeps it to itself.

(Most Ghia owners had VW's first and knew just what they were getting.)

Inside you'll find all those little things you've told yourself you'd put in a car if you were the factory.

Bucket seats with backs you can adjust. A door with stops to hold it in 3 different positions.

A defroster for the rear window.

Even a soundproofed interior, with an acoustical ceiling like a modern office. If you hear a siren in the distance, pull over. It's right behind you.

Now then, how much?

$2,395* for the coupe, $2,595* for the convertible. Heater, electric clock and all.

Sorry we can't do anything about strangers who think it's a $5,000 car. You may still find bellboys and doormen expecting bigger tips.

But nothing's ever perfect, is it?

The Karmann-Ghia story was not told in national ads in the United States until 1961, which is amazing since fifty percent of all Ghias are exported—eighty percent of them to the United States.

You'd lose.

The racy-looking car in the picture would have trouble beating a Volkswagen.

Because it is a Volkswagen. Inside.

Outside it's a Karmann Ghia.

A Karmann Ghia isn't really a racing car. Though it is custom-built like one.

Its lines are too sculptured for mass production.

The front fender, for instance, has to be formed in three sections. Then ground down, filed and sanded. All by hand.

But beneath that wanton exterior beats a heart of Volkswagen.

Same engine, same chassis, same transmission. Which means same reliability, same economy, same service.

We know a Ghia can't do much at the Sebring road races.

But it can cruise at 72, corner like a sports car, and hold the road like one.

And it might comfort you to know, you'd be driving the best-made loser on the track.

An example of 1962 advertising.

had arrived as part of a German trade show in New York in 1949. They attracted the eye of Max Hoffman, erstwhile import dealer, the man who established dozens of European makes in America after the war. Hoffman approached VW's Heinz Nordhoff for the VW concession in 1950—and was offered the whole company for two million dollars.

Saying no to that offer, as he later admitted, was Max's first major mistake. He did like the Beetle, though, so Nordhoff made Hoffman the exclusive American VW importer; the first consignment of cars arriving in July 1950. Hoffman's Beetles, however, refused to sell. Through 1953 Hoffman Motors never moved more than 1,000 units per year. "I tried and I tried hard," Hoffman said, "but I just could not do it." In late 1953 Nordhoff let the contract lapse and Hoffman got out of the VW business for good. That was Max's second mistake.

Also in 1953, Nordhoff had asked Arthur Stanton, a successful American exporter working out of Morocco, to return to the States and report on the potential market for Volkswagens. Stanton thought the company had a future in America, but recommended a complete overhaul of the sales operation. He suggested two sales areas, with the Mississippi River as the arbitrary dividing line. The western area went to prominent sports car importer John von Neumann, while Stanton took on the East under the umbrella of World-Wide Automobiles Corp., Long Island City, New York.

von Neumann and Stanton signed up a few dealers and distributors. Convinced now that VW could indeed sell cars in America, Heinz Nordhoff dispatched courtly, handsome Will van de Kamp to supervise the overall picture, and VW really began to roll.

"Will van de Kamp was an evangelist, possessed of a near-fanatic missionary zeal," wrote Walter H. Nelson in his VW history, *Small Wonder*. ". . . he never doubted for a second that Volkswagen would become a tremendous success in the United States." It was van de Kamp who hired a bright twenty-five-year-old Englishman, J. Stuart Perkins, to help him set up VW's American headquarters in New York in June 1955. Initially called Volkswagen United States, this firm soon evolved into Volkswagen of America Inc., a wholly-owned subsidiary of Volkswagenwerk and sole importer of VWs for the U.S.

This was the critical background, not only behind the Beetle's sudden transformation from fringe model to number one import, but behind the emergence of the Karmann-Ghia. For both van de Kamp and Perkins were sure, as they told Nordhoff, that the Ghia-styled two-seater Volkswagen had a definite future in the U.S. market.

One of the earliest Karmann-Ghia press releases was distributed under the letterhead of Stanton's World-Wide Automobiles in 1956. It dubbed the Ghia "Volkswagen's stylish young sister," and noted that it had already become "one of the most popular [two-seat] coupes in America, second only to the Chevrolet Corvette." That statement was peculiar on several counts. The Corvette was really an *open* sports car (the Ghia convertible was still two years off), though in 1956 it could be ordered with a lift-off hardtop. Also, neither the Ghia nor Corvette rivaled the Ford Thunderbird in sales—although the Bird, too, was essentially an open two-seater.

1955 coupe.

Thunderbird helpfully abandoned the two-seater market in 1958, and it is interesting to observe how the sales of both Karmann-Ghia and Corvette improved after that happened.

Year	Corvette	Karmann-Ghia	Thunderbird
1956	3,388	2,452	15,631
1957	6,246	4,130	21,380
1958	9,168	6,025	
1959	9,670	8,035	
1960	10,261	9,291	

The Karmann-Ghia's slow start in America really had more to do with Karmann's ability to produce cars than with any reluctance on the part of van de Kamp, Perkins and company. Its European reception had

1958 convertible.

been equally positive—yet in 1956 Karmann was turning out only 300-400 Ghias a month for the worldwide market, just half of which were earmarked for the U.S. By 1957 it was up to 1,000 per month, but even then the order backlog was so deep that most U.S. dealers were quoting two- to four-year waits for delivery. "We were taking ten percent deposits and posting the waiting list in the showroom," remembers one VW dealer. "Hardly anybody dropped out and asked for their money back, and the waiting lists just kept growing. It was the first time we'd experienced anything like that."

The fact, borne out by the Karmann-Ghia's spiraling sales from its very first year, is that the Italianesque two-seater gave Volkswagen of America an outstanding secondary product. Most observers predicted this from the beginning. Despite getting its name backward, for example, *Road & Track* forecast certain success in its 1956 road test: "If looks are paramount, there is little doubt that [the Ghia] will find fertile soil. The VW-GK [sic] . . . has an almost universal appeal to the eye. It is, as the French would say, *une poupée vivante.*"

Most testers noticed that driving a Karmann-Ghia was not at all like pushing a conventional Beetle. The same rear-mounted eggbeater four, the slick four-speed gearbox, the leisurely acceleration and soul-testing final oversteer were all there, of course. But the driver sat lower, at a more relaxed angle, the legs stretched out, the steering wheel a bit farther away from the chest. Visibility was outstanding in every direction, thanks to Ghia's ultra-slim roof pillars and generous expanse of glass, and each car was finished to gem-like perfection by the elves of Osnabrück.

Naturally the early Ghias were criticized in America for the same faults as the Beetles were: the lack of a fuel gauge (this was corrected early on the Karmann-Ghia, by 1958), inadequate cockpit ventilation, a fair amount of noise at speed and a heating system bereft of huff-and-puff. Admittedly the latter problem was less severe in Ghias than Beetles, for there was a lot less interior to heat. But it still took time and fairly high rpm to get the system perking on cold mornings.

Another unfortunate characteristic, peculiar to the Karmann-Ghia alone, had to do with its method of construction. Myriad joints and seams filled with English pewter shaped with beachwood tools sounds very exotic

For people who can't stand the sight of a Volkswagen.

Some people just can't see a VW.

Even though they admire its attributes, they picture themselves in something fancier.

We sell such a package.

It's called a Karmann Ghia.

The Karmann Ghia is what happened to a Volkswagen when an Italian designer got hold of it.

He didn't design it for mass production, so we wouldn't think of giving it the mass production treatment.

We take time to hand-weld, hand-shape, and hand-smooth the body.

Finally, after 185 men have had a hand in it, the Ghia's body is lowered onto one of those strictly functional chassis.

The kind that comes with VW's big 15-inch wheels, torsion bars, our 4-speed synchromesh transmission and that rather famous air-cooled engine.

So that along with its Roman nose and graceful curves, the Ghia has a beauty that is more than skin deep.

In 1964, Volkswagen in America, Inc., ran this ad in *Road & Track*.

What if you put Volkswagen parts in a Karmann Ghia?

They'd fit.

Even if one of the parts was the engine. Because the engine is a VW engine. And the transmission and chassis are Volkswagen's, too.

Which makes the Ghia one of the best-humored runabouts on the road.

And one of the easiest to service.

If you're in a strange town, just ask any cop for the nearest Volkswagen dealer.)

But let us tell you about the body. It takes 185 men to make this body.

It was designed by Ghia of Turin but was too sculptured for mass production.

So we farm the Ghia out to one of Europe's finest custom coachworks, Karmann of Osnabruck. Where the body is welded, ground down, filed and sanded —all by hand.

The VW Karmann Ghia comes with bucket seats with backs you can adjust. Acoustical soundproofing like an office. Electric clock. Even a defroster for the rear window.

People accustomed to a little posh usually guess the Ghia's price at around $5,000. Pish posh. The coupé's only $2,295.* the convertible $2,495.*

The advertising campaign for 1965 included this piece.

in sales brochures. (One U.S. flyer actually suggested that "no two Ghias are ever exactly alike!") But it also implied a chronic rust problem, particularly when the cars were subjected to the heavily salted winter roads of North America. This difficulty was never really licked because it was endemic to the breed, and is the reason low-mileage Ghias, or examples from "rust-free" areas like California and central Florida, are so highly prized by collectors today.

There was little difference between the Bug and the Ghia in acceleration, but most testers obtained rather better top speeds in the two-seater, thanks to its superior streamlining; and this was important in a nation of super-highways. *Road & Track* even thought that the acceleration was better. "We have never been able to induce a stock VW sedan to break 70 mph for a timed 4-way average or beat 30 secs. from the 0-to-60," the editors wrote, "and we have tried a good many. The GK [sic], thanks to streamlining, will finally do the trick. Its best run was almost 78 mph (indicating 83) and its best 0-60, 27.7 secs."

Such advantages were of course incremental compared to the standard Beetle. People probably *felt* a lot quicker in the Ghia than they really were, simply because it looked so smooth and felt so "right" from behind the wheel. But underneath the fancy dress it remained a VW, with all that implied. This is where the modifiers got busy.

After the Beetle had become a cult car, hotted-up Bugs were commonplace; but many of the early tuning jobs in America were done on Karmann-Ghias. Americans favored at least four methods of rendering Ghia performance on a par with its looks. The least expensive, provided you did the installation yourself, was the combination of high-compression pistons and special-grind camshaft, which were offered by numerous after-market suppliers. These gave a marked improvement in performance, with the 1200 cc Ghias sprinting from 0-60 in 23-24 seconds, giving a genuine 80 mph top speed; the 1300, 1500 and 1600 cc models were commensurately faster.

At the other end of the scale, some Americans actually installed Porsche engines. Most Porsche-swaps came from junkyard 356's, but there were people abroad in the land, remarkably enough, who engineered the switch "from now." One of these purchased a brand new Karmann-Ghia

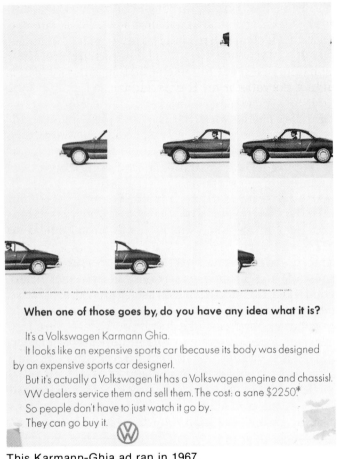

When one of those goes by, do you have any idea what it is?

It's a Volkswagen Karmann Ghia.

It looks like an expensive sports car (because its body was designed by an expensive sports car designer).

But it's actually a Volkswagen (it has a Volkswagen engine and chassis). VW dealers service them and sell them. The cost: a sane $2250*

So people don't have to just watch it go by.

They can go buy it.

This Karmann-Ghia ad ran in 1967.

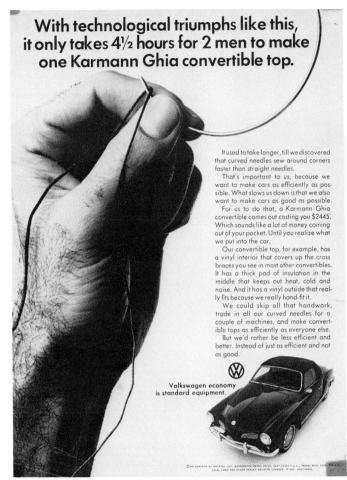

With technological triumphs like this, it only takes 4½ hours for 2 men to make one Karmann Ghia convertible top.

It used to take longer, till we discovered that curved needles sew around corners faster than straight needles.

That's important to us, because we want to make cars as efficiently as possible. What slows us down is that we also want to make cars as good as possible.

For us to do that, a Karmann Ghia convertible comes out costing you $2445. Which sounds like a lot of money coming out of your pocket. Until you realize what we put into the car.

Our convertible top, for example, has a vinyl interior that covers up the cross braces you see in most other convertibles. It has a thick pad of insulation in the middle that keeps out heat, cold and noise. And it has a vinyl outside that really fits because we really hand-fit it.

We could skip all that handwork, trade in all our curved needles for a couple of machines, and make convertible tops as efficiently as everyone else.

But we'd rather be less efficient and better. Instead of just as efficient and not as good.

Volkswagen economy is standard equipment.

One of the more innovative ads from Doyle Dane Bernbach.

from a Pennsylvania dealer in 1965, having arranged to "turn in" the new engine for a rebate. This he used as down payment on a new 1600 cc Porsche "normal" engine, which naturally transformed the behavior of his Ghia. His total investment was over $5,000 at a time when the standard Karmann-Ghia sold under $3,000. One had to marvel at his determination, since $5,000 in those days almost bought a Corvette or an E-type Jaguar.

One of the middling performance routes was the Okrasa tuning kit, built in Germany and sole in the late fifties and sixties for about $250-300. The essential component here was special cylinder heads and related parts, providing 7.5:1 compression without the need for high-compression pistons. The kit gave better cooling, provided room for larger intake valves, and allowed larger, un-siamesed ports. Okrasas added 10 mph to the Ghia's top speed and provided 70 mph from rest in the time stock models required for 60 mph. The quarter mile took about three seconds less, and horsepower went from 36 to 46, a solid thirty percent gain. Torque increased eighteen percent from fifty-six to sixty-six pounds-feet. *Road & Track* said the Okrasa-Ghia "idles the same, sounds the same, feels the same. Yet anyone who owns and drives a normal VW will know instantly that something is different." The magazine's only objection was that Okrasa-equipped cars were "too easy and too tempting to over-rev."

Roots-type superchargers by firms like Judson or M.A.G. were also available for Ghias, though reliability was a problem in the experience of many owners. Blown 1100s would run 0-60 in about twenty seconds, and higher-displacement Ghias would do it in regular sports car time. A big boost in mid-range torque improved top gear pickup and helped eliminate the characteristic wide step between second and third gears. Blower kits were expensive, however, and also offered the temptation to ask more of the engine than it was capable of delivering.

Once VW of America had been assured an adequate supply of the little charmer, it asked its famous ad agency, Doyle Dane Bernbach, to apply its inimitable talents to a Ghia ad campaign. "In the last 6 years this car has mystified millions," read the agency's lead-off layout in 1961. "People have called it everything from an Alfa Romeo to a Ferrari . . . Brace yourself. It's a Volkswagen."

Doyle Dane Bernbach must have been waiting for a pretty VW for years. It was perfect for the agency—just the sort of contradiction in terms that fit its droll advertising style. One early spread suggested that the Ghia was ideal "For people who can't stand the sight of a Volkswagen." Another, picturing a Ghia coupe with racing stripes and numbers, remarked, "The car in the picture would have trouble beating a Volkswagen."

It got wilder: "There's a little bug in every Karmann-Ghia" and "What if you put Volkswagen parts in a Karmann-Ghia? [They'd fit.]" reminded people of the utterly reliable underpinnings of the handsome two-seaters. The agency radiated that inverse snob appeal which had made the Beetle ads famous. Picturing five identical macho types in dark glasses, driving convertibles by Porsche, Ferrari, Mercedes, Jaguar, and the Karmann-Ghia, it asked the reader, "Can you spot the druggist from Toledo?" That ad, wrote Frank Rowsome, Jr., "did not so much offer up paens of praise of sheet metal as make the down-to-earth observation that it was not necessary to pay Ferrari prices to have an elegant car . . . As in other VW ads, a tartness in viewing the general automotive scene was evident.

Volkswagen hesitated for some time before entering television marketing. But TV had become the dominant American media by the sixties, and the use of it was inevitable. Doyle Dane Bernbach duly produced TV spots in the same spirit of whimsy as its magazine layouts. One Karmann-Ghia ad became famous in the advertising world. Taking aim at the legion of auto commercials showing cars breaking through paper barriers, the agency delighted audiences by showing a Karmann-Ghia repeatedly nudging but failing to penetrate its paper barrier. "The Volkswagen Karmann-Ghia is the most economical sports car you can buy," went the accompanying dialogue—"It's just not the most powerful."

Volkswagen of America persistently sold the Ghia image as an elegant, quality two-seater with total reliability, serviceable by any VW store. Never did they issue a high-performance version, despite a contemporary market teeming with "muscle cars," "ponycars" and family sedans converted to "GTs" via racing stripes and walnut shift knobs. It was a sound philosophy—keeping the Ghia out of the competitive performance-car ruck, while carving out a loyal market where there was no competition. (The only possible rival was Renault's Caravelle, but this suffered the same reliability problems as its parent Dauphine, and disappeared with the latter in 1967, having made no dent on Karmann-Ghia sales.)

Even after the federal government forced VW to mess up the design (vision-obstructing high-back seats and ugly side-markers in 1968, gross looking girder bumpers in 1972), Ghia enthusiasts continued to buy and enjoy their Pussycats. The charming Ghia had indeed won many hearts. In 1972, *Car and Driver* went so far as to compare it with that greatest of rear-engined cult cars, the Porsche Speedster, telling its readers "to accept the fact that the last Speedster built is a Karmann-Ghia."

The Ghia, *Car and Driver* admitted, needed a bolt-on tach and a few adjustments to the seat mountings to invoke the Speedster feeling. But the dimensional and performance comparisons were extremely close. By 1972 the Ghia had progressed to 1584 cc, nearly identical to the Speedster's 1582. It still gave away 10 hp to the Porsche, but it was only a second and 4 mph slower in the quarter mile, and in handling and braking tests the Ghia "devastated the Speedster." About the only thing the Karmann-Ghia didn't provide, *Car and Driver* decided, was close ratios between second and third gears—and you could alleviate that problem with a multitude of carb, manifold and exhaust kits.

By 1972, though, the epic journey of the Karmann-Ghia was fast winding up, in America as elsewhere. For the first time in six years U.S. sales fell below 20,000, and continued to drop through 1974, the Ghia's last year. This was not due to any decrease in American demand, but rather to the revolutionary changes occurring at Wolfsburg: the advent of the front-wheel-drive, watercooled Rabbit and *its* sporty derivation, the Scirocco. A new age was dawning, and in Volkswagenwerk's formula for it, the Karmann-Ghia no longer figured.

Its styling was perceptibly aging by then, of course. And the Americans had done their bit to pollute the original, almost faultless design. Emission controls had countered whatever performance improvements might have been gained through larger-displacement engines. But none of these factors was significant enough in itself to make Americans give up the Pussycat. They gave up only because the supply stopped.

KARMANN-GHIA U.S. SALES BY MODEL YEAR

Year	143 Coupe	141 Conv.	1432 Coupe*	1412 Conv.*	Total
1956	2,452	--	--	--	2,452
1957	4,130	--	--	--	4,130
1958	[4,700]	[1,325]	--	--	6,025
1959	[6,265]	[1,770]	--	--	8,035
1960	[7,247]	[2,044]	--	--	9,291
1961	[6,706]	[1,891]	--	--	8,597
1962	[9,565]	[2,723]	--	--	12,379
1963	[12,010]	[3,387]	--	--	15,397
1964	[13,084]	[3,691]	--	--	16,775
1965	[14,191]	[4,003]	--	--	18,194
1966	[17,112]	[4,827]	--	--	21,939
1967	16,107	3,174	--	--	19,281
1968	14,600	3,075	4,577	1,082	23,334
1969	16,652	3,507	4,448	1,077	25,684
1970	21,520	**	11,432	5,873	38,825
1971	17,816	5,567	***	***	23,383
1972	11,208	3,076	***	***	14,284
1973	10,271	2,650	***	***	12,921
1974	5,779	1,926	***	***	7,705

* automatic stick-shift
** listed under #1432 in 1970
*** included in 143/141 totals
[] brackets indicate estimates for coupe vs. convertible based on the 1967-73 breakdown of 78% coupes, 22% convertibles. Separate figures not available.

Source: Volkswagen of America Inc.

KARMANN-GHIA BASE PRICES IN U.S.
(EAST COAST; WEST COAST ADD $100-150)

Year	143 Coupe	141 Conv.	1432 Coupe*	1412 Conv.*
1956	$2395	--	--	--
1957	2395	--	--	--
1958	2445	$2725	--	--
1959	2445	2725	--	--
1960	2430	2695	--	--
1961	2430	2695	--	--
1962	2295	2495	--	--
1963	2295	2495	--	--
1964	2295	2495	--	--
1965	2295	2495	--	--
1966	2235	2428	--	--
1967	2250	2445	--	--
1968	2254	2449	$2389	$2584
1969	2365	2575	2504	2714
1970	2399	2609	2538	2748
1971	2575	2750	2714	2889
1972	2750	3099	2889	3238
1973	3050	3450	3189	3589
1974	3475	3935	3750	4210

* automatic

Source: N.A.D.A. Used Car Guides, 1961-75.

Bibliography.

Clarke, R. M. (Ed.): *VW Karmann Ghia*, Brooklands, Surrey UK 1982
Fry, Robin: *The VW Beetle*, David & Charles, London 1980
Hopfinger, K. B.: *The Volkswagen Story*, Robt. Bentley, Cambridge 1971
Ludvigsen, Karl: "The Baron of Park Avenue" [Max Hoffman], *Automobile Quarterly*, Second Quarter 1972
Nelson, Walter H.: *Small Wonder*, Little Brown, Boston 1967
Post, Dan R.: *Volkswagen/Nine Lives Later*, Horizon, Arcadia CA 1966
Rowsome, Frank Jr.: *Think Small*, Stephen Greene, Brattleboro VT 1970
Autocar, Car and Driver, Road & Track: contemporary issues
Car Collector (1981), *Cars & Parts* (1972): articles by Richard M. Langworth

APPENDIX

Rally champ.

A would-be virtuoso has to start practicing young. While the prototype KdF car was still undergoing road trials there were opportunities to test performance in motor sporting events. One of these was the Berlin—Rome—Berlin long distance drive which was to lead across the Alps in the autumn. Dr. Porsche developed three VW Type 60 streamlined coupés for the event. Their Porsche engines developed 32 bhp instead of the standard 24 bhp, allowing the vehicles to attain a top speed of 130 km/h.

The effort was however all for nought. The war's outbreak brought all plans to an abrupt halt.

Then around 1950 after motor sport had struggled back onto its feet during the hard post war years, many a Beetle enthusiast was happy to participate vigorously in rallies and races. Large wheels, short wheelbase, high ground clearance and a sturdy body made the Beetle every bit the equal of rough ground.

It is true that no comprehensive statistics exist on Beetle rally successes but the large number of victories in Germany and abroad speaks for itself. For instance, in 1973 four Type 1302 S and 1303 S Beetles caused a stir. They were tuned by Volkswagen-Porsche in Salzburg and driven by experienced drivers. They soon were figuring as favourites in international rallies all across Europe, as at the 6th International Elba Rally which led over 1,500 km of gravel tracks and sprint tests in rough terrain. The team of Achim Warmbold (Germany) and Gunnar Haggbom (Sweden) drove off with the overall victory. Of the rally's 90 starters 68 did not even finish.

The victorious car had heavy duty bumpers and its engine and gearbox were shielded against stone knocks. The output of the 1.6 litre engine had been upped by the Volkswagen-Porsche tuners from the standard 50 bhp to 126 bhp.

The 1974 New Caledonia Safari Rally provided another opportunity for the Beetle to show what it could do. The 4,000 km long course included all sorts of difficult terrain. The rally was won by a Beetle with a completely unmodified 54 bhp engine.

The only change was reinforcement of the vehicle floor with aluminium sheets to endure bumps and stone knocks when fording streams.

For the sake of curiousity mention is also made of a super Beetle, a phantom which in 1973 haunted the Hanover area not all too far away

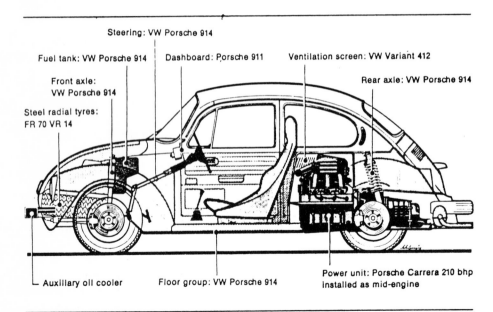

Steering: VW Porsche 914

Fuel tank: VW Porsche 914   Dashboard: Porsche 911   Ventilation screen: VW Variant 412

Front axle:
VW Porsche 914   Rear axle: VW Porsche 914

Steel radial tyres:
FR 70 VR 14

Auxiliary oil cooler   Floor group: VW Porsche 914   Power unit: Porsche Carrera 210 bhp
installed as mid-engine

Factory information on VWs in competition.

from V-n's main plant in Wolfsburg. Workers at the Nordstadt dealership had worked with energy and enthusiasm to develop a one-of-a-kind Beetle and secure its licensing as roadworthy. The recipe: taking the floor group including running gear, racing wheels and steel radial tyres of the VW-Porsche 914, one installs the Porsche Carrera's power unit as a mid-engine and covers everything up with a Beetle 1303 body. Around 2,000 hours of hard work went into the project. The resulting juggernaut achieved a top speed of 213 km/h thanks to its 2.7 litre, 210 bhp engine. And so every now and again the users of Lower Saxony's autobahns became witness to a wonder: an innocuous looking Beetle would suddenly accelerate and effortlessly pass over-heavy high output cars, thus revealing itself as a "Wolfsburger" in sheeps clothing.

Volkswagen was also ready to stand godfather when in 1962 the American VW dealer Hubert Brundage had the absurd idea of installing a Beetle engine in his own small racecar. Another American, Air Force Colonel Smith, took up the concept. In Nardi in Italy he had his own personal one-seater built from Genuine Volkswagen Parts.

In 1963 this new Beetle-based racecar type was approved by racing authorities, whereupon Dr. Ferry Porsche, son and successor of Prof. Ferdinand Porsche, the Volkswagen's creator, introduced the new racecar in Europe amidst general enthusiasm. The Formula V (= Volkswagen) racecar began its triumphal tour which has permitted young racecar drivers the world over to break into professional racing without inordinate cost.

Roughly 7,800 Formula V one-seaters have been built to date. This is in itself an unofficial record: the world's highest production of Formula racecars.

Of course not all Beetle fans wanted to contend with the rigorous requirements of Formula V racing. Again it was the decendents of the tamers of the Wild West who, with their drive for open spaces, sought out new rugged courses well off the beaten track: straight across country, out in the open nature far from human habitation. The dune buggies were created, along with other open air cars. Soon there wasn't a desert, a beach or a sandune in Nevada, California or Arizona that was safe from invasion.

People held ralleys to pit their strength and driving skill against improvised competitors. Amidst the throng of motoring adventurists which formed when these enthusiasts got together, the Jeeps among the crowd looked like harmless civilians.

Since 1967 the most demanding competition of this sort, the "Baja 1,000", has been held on the Mexican peninsula of Baja California over a course where one is more likely to see a rattlesnake than a tree. 80 % of all vehicles competing are built using VW parts. Two of the nine classes of starting vehicles are reserved exclusively for VW modifications. As suppliers of sturdy, inexpensive parts Beetles play a significant role — both for the front axle and for the rear axle, generally with over-sized tyres. The whole thing is held together by a criss-cross pipe frame of some sort, a sturdy construction which takes no account of its own weight. The frame keeps the sandflea from coming apart even when it lands hard after one of its frequent jumps for joy.

INDEX